Two for Charging

A SECOND CHANCE COLLEGE HOCKEY ROMANCE

LASAIRIONA MCMASTER

DRAMA LLAMA PUBLISHING

Copyright © 2022 by Lasairiona McMaster

The moral right of Lasairiona McMaster to be identified as the author of this work has been asserted in accordance with the copyright, designs, and patents act of 1988.

All rights reserved.

No part of this book may be reproduced in any form or by any electronic or mechanical means, including information storage and retrieval systems, without written permission from the author, except for the use of brief quotations in a book review. Your support for the Author's rights is appreciated.

All the characters in this book are fictitious and any resemblance to actual persons living or dead, are purely coincidental.

Dedication

For all the moms out there—doing all the things, all the time.
This one's for you.
I see you.
You are enough.
You are a good mom.
And yes, the laundry can wait until tomorrow.
Give them the damned screen, take a load off, and treat yourself
to a couple hours' peace.
You've more than earned it.

CHAPTER 1
Clare

"Regular flow or heavy?" Clare pursed her lips and regarded the selection of care products in front of her. "What a total crock of shit."

No matter how bright and attractive companies made the packaging, a period still felt like a sucker punch to the uterus.

By a bear.

With a fucking jackhammer.

There was no way to make that shit cute. Period products *lied*. No one was that chipper when Aunt Flo came to visit. And if they were, they were probably a serial killer... Because they had their fucking period.

If they offered a "swamp witch" variety of Tampax, however, she'd hand them her PIN number in a flash. A haggard woman shoveling a gallon of ice cream into her pimpletastic face while crying over every teeny tiny little thing and shitting through the eye of a goddamn needle. Period poop was no fucking joke.

She swiped a packet from the shelf and waved it high above her head. "Cat? Regular or heavy?"

Silence. Her nineteen-year-old daughter was nowhere to

be seen. Maybe she'd gone back out to the car. Or maybe she was hiding behind a display of Lindor chocolate balls, pretending she was in no way related to the wild woman muttering to herself about periods and pads.

Fine. If her dearest darling daughter was embarrassed by her, she'd double down. She grabbed one of each, regular, heavy, and overnight pads, and snagged regular and heavy tampons for good measure.

Humming *Sisters Are Doin' it for Themselves* by Eurythmics, she inched toward the end of the aisle.

The benefit of having the Leaning Tower of Period Products stacked high in her arms was that she couldn't reach the shelf of Lindor balls. Or carry any chocolate at all for that matter. A fact her fast tightening jeans would thank her for.

She'd let herself go since the divorce. She wasn't one of those women who'd caught her husband cheating on her and used it to drop twenty pounds and fuel some rage-filled magic makeover.

The only thing it had fueled was depression, self-loathing, and a need to buy bigger pants. And the only thing she'd dropped was her self-respect.

"Asshole." She glared at the Lindor chocolate like it was the one who had banged their secretary on the family dining table and not her piece-of-shit ex.

Rounding the end of the aisle, she crashed into something, her body tensing as the collision knocked the air out of her. The pads and tampons flew from her arms like someone had pulled out a wooden Jenga block from her carefully crafted and precariously balanced tower.

"Oof! Sorry." Her muttered apology was aimed at the sneakers of the person she'd bumped into as she bent over to pick up her fallen spoils with a weighty sigh.

That's what she got for trying to embarrass her daughter. Apparently Karma worked fast when it was against her. If only it would work as quickly on her ex—maybe give him a raging case of crabs, or remove all the labels from the cans of food in his pantry.

Ha! If only.

The body in front of her didn't move, so she abandoned the period product recovery plan in favor of shooing off the person looming over her. She'd said sorry, what else could Mr. Bootcut Jeans want?

As she straightened, the back of her head connected with something hard and she winced. Pain rippled across her scalp. She hadn't even planned on stopping at CVS on her way home, but Catriona was desperate and now it was a thing.

But based on how the pharmacy was going, dinner would be drive-thru Panera. Relatively healthy and minimal peopleing. If the car found its way into the drive-thru at Taco Bell, she wouldn't be mad about it.

"Sorry. Here. Let me." A gravelly voice that sent tingles all the way to her toes instantly cured her brewing concussion. A firm grip banded around her bicep, helping her straighten up. All the oxygen evaporated from her body.

"Elliott." His name caught in her throat, croaking like it had been trapped there for decades. It kind of had.

The boy she'd once loved was all man now. Square jaw covered with a neat, dark, salt-and-pepper beard that her fingers itched to reach out and stroke. Small crow's feet crinkling the corners of his eyes. Brown, wavy hair, still styled with gel but with a dusting of gray at the temples.

He'd aged well. Too well.

Clare knew those hazel eyes. She'd stared into them when she'd pressed a sweater against his face after he'd taken a stray puck to the eyebrow in a game of street hockey when he was a kid. She'd stared at them over numerous games of cribbage in her backyard. It had taken her a while to get used to the card game with the little peg stand, but once she'd mastered counting points in combinations of fifteens, it was on like *Donkey Kong*.

She'd pleaded with them when he'd told her he was going to be leaving and pursuing his dreams. Those hazel eyes were burned into her memory forever.

She'd heard he was coaching the local college hockey team. Sure, he had a little squish around his middle underneath his solid black t-shirt—probably from moving into coaching rather than still playing—but he was still every bit Elliott.

Her Elliott.

She swallowed down the bitter taste in her mouth. He wasn't hers anymore. Perhaps he never had been.

He'd done good things with the team, great, in fact. If she wasn't still pissed at him she'd be proud of him. Her heart twisted. She was always proud of him.

She smoothed her hand over her not-been-washed-in-a-week hair, face aflame, and gave an awkward laugh. "Elliott."

Why did her voice sound so... weird?

His eyebrows were arched high. His jaw hung open. The golden-brown circle around the pupil in his left eye caught the light as his gaze bore into hers, as though searching for something. Mute.

Silently urging him to speak, she slid her damp palms over the thighs of her yoga pants. Had she let herself go so much that he didn't even recognize her? Or was he simply stunned at the fact she was wearing yesterday's *Feminist AF* shirt?

Okay, so her toothpaste had splattered on it a bit, but it kind of looked like it was supposed to be that way, so she'd just gone with it. Another tuck of her hair behind her ear, another awkward giggle.

"Okay. Um." She gestured at the boxes and packets on the ground and crouched to pick them up, careful to avoid another collision against...well...any part of him.

As though her bending snapped him out of whatever daze

he was in, he squatted in front of her, scrambling to pick up the boxes.

Definitely Karma. His thighs filled out his jeans like he'd been poured into the denim. Was it weird to want to bite someone's thigh? She wasn't sure she cared.

His eyes were still on her when they stood again. He offered her the heavy flow and overnight pads with a raised eyebrow. His lips twitched like he fought a smile.

Her face was on fire. No, she wasn't lucky enough to be on fire. But the heat of her cheeks could most definitely have started one. "They're for my daughter."

Fan-fucking-tastic. Now he probably thought her daughter was having some kind of severe period emergency that required almost forty pads and the same number of tampons.

Closing her eyes for a beat, Clare sucked in an audible breath through her nose. Maybe if she didn't meet his confused, amused, and bottomless gaze she'd be able to jump-start her brain with the heat radiating from the rest of her body.

If only wishing made it so.

When she opened her eyes, he was still there, head canted, smile teasing at the corners of his lips. She pinned her stare to the center of his chest, but couldn't make her feet move away from him.

He was still voiceless, and she was stuck. Two decades ago they'd have dissolved into a fit of laughter over the whole thing. But now? Their history stretched out between them like taffy in summer heat in the heavy silence.

Too much history. Too much time.

Swallowing down the lump forming in her throat, she turned toward the counter and strode away with purpose. Every fiber of her being wanted to abandon Operation Shark Week and flee the state, but Catriona needed provisions. Plus, if she ran, he'd totally know she was rattled.

Hell, he probably already knew. He always had known her better than she even knew herself. But she wasn't going to let him see it. Forcing a smile for the cashier, she paid for her items and waved off the receipt. Who needed to take proof of the dreaded *pink tax* home with them?

Who needed to carry around a record of such an inordinate spend on something that cost mere pennies to make? Especially for shit that damn near every woman of a certain age needed.

Was she deflecting the fact Elliott's burning gaze still pierced her back at the checkout with ire at Proctor and Gamble? Maybe.

Did she pick up a packet of gum, two Snickers, and a bag of Sour Patch Kids for a second transaction to buy time so she could pull her shit together before turning to face him again? Damn straight she did.

Hopefully if she took long enough at the checkout, when she turned around, he'd magically be gone. A hallucination. A figment of her imagination conjured to remind her that despite being screwed over by her asshole ex, she was still a woman, still had needs. She was divorced for crying out loud, not dead.

He cleared his throat as she declined the second receipt. No such luck. She shoved the candy into her mom-bag. Either she'd find them again in a month or two in a moment of dire snack-emergency, or Catriona would find them and remove the temptation when she next *borrowed* twenty bucks.

She thanked the cashier with a tight-lipped smile.

The young woman, whose name tag was hidden by her jacket, leaned forward, jerking her chin at Elliott, and lowered her voice. "Ma'am, is that guy bothering you?"

Clare snorted, almost choking on her own tongue, but

shook her head. "No, we're old friends. Thanks for looking out for me though."

The young woman didn't seem convinced, but she nodded. "We get some weirdos around here sometimes."

Was she calling Elliott the weirdo, or her? Either way, she wasn't wrong.

"Clare?"

She spun to face him. "Elliott." Yup. She'd said nothing but his name to him, three times and counting. While she might have enjoyed how her tongue felt around it, he probably already knew his own name.

An uncertain smile spread across his face as he opened his arms. Was he going to hug her? Cheese and crackers, hell no. If he did that, she'd be forced to feel him all around her, and she might do something even more embarrassing than covering him in boxes of Tampax...like...sniff him. Did he still smell of soap?

She held up her two bags as though they were enough of an explanation as to why she couldn't return his hug.

"Long time." His sad eyes almost made her want to drop her bags and throw herself into his arms.

Almost.

"Yeah. Long time." It was the understatement of the century, but she nodded.

"How are you? You look good."

And he was still a lying liar who lied. He told her he wouldn't leave to play hockey. And when he did, he told her he'd come back. He never came back.

A zebra never changed its stripes. Or whatever the hell the thing about people never changing was. Clearly his presence still fucked up her ability to think straight.

"You too."

He tucked his hands into his back pockets and rocked

back on his heels like an *aw shucks* teenager asking a girl out for the first time.

She almost laughed. "Well, I better get going." She lifted her bags again. Another reminder of the Big Red Emergency. Peachy.

All she needed to do to complete her mortification, was to trip over thin air and land on her face as she left.

"Clare?"

She was almost at the door before that voice crashed into her again, stopping her in her tracks and warming her all over.

That was her name, don't wear it out. Pausing, she turned her chin over her shoulder, but he didn't say anything else. She turned a little more, enough to see his brows knit into a frown and a huge sigh escape him.

He tossed her a half-shrug. "It was good to see you."

Liar. A pap smear would have been more enjoyable, and he didn't even have a fucking cervix. Rolling her lips between her teeth in a bid to stop a salty response from breaking free, she nodded. "You too."

She sank into the driver's seat of her car and tossed the bag over her shoulder into the back seat. Then she slammed the door. She wouldn't cry. She wouldn't look at the door to CVS because he'd undoubtedly be standing there, watching her hot mess self having a nervous breakdown at seeing him.

She was pulling out of the parking lot when movement in the rearview mirror caught her attention. Catriona stood at the entrance to the drugstore, waving both her hands like she was stranded at sea and flagging down a rescue.

Clare slammed on the brakes. She'd forgotten her fucking daughter. Though the way the kid stood swinging her hands over her head was testament to the fact she had indeed been hiding inside the building and ignoring Clare's hollering outright.

Jerking the door to the passenger seat open, Catriona

erupted into a fit of giggles. "I can't believe you were going to drive off without me, Mom."

"And I can't believe you hid in the drugstore and pretended I wasn't asking you questions about your period products."

The mother of all eye rolls preceded a tut. "I can't believe you were asking me questions about my period products in a voice that was not what anyone would have considered a suitable indoor voice."

It was her turn to eye roll. There was no mistaking where her kid got her sassitude from.

"Know what else I can't believe, Mom?"

Clare quirked her brow as she pulled out of the parking lot for the second time.

"I can't believe you're just driving home as though we're going to ignore the fact you were just talking to a hottie in the drugstore. Well." She held up a palm before another fit of giggles hit. "I don't think we could really call that talking, can we?"

Clare groaned. They were not having that conversation. "I need to concentrate on the road."

"Right. That would be a first." An indignant snort rang from her kid as the light at the intersection changed to red.

"Shit."

"Nice try. You don't need to concentrate on the road when we're sitting still, do you, Mom? Spill. Tell me *everything* about the hunky silver fox makin' eyes at you over tampons at the store."

Silver fox? They weren't that old, were they? Dear Jesus in the manger, please tell her they weren't at silver fox age quite yet.

"He's just someone I used to know." Her fingers tapped on the steering wheel as her glare bored into the red light hanging in front of her.

"How?" Catriona tore open a box of Whoppers and dropped a couple into her mouth.

"School." The traitorous light was still red, and a sidelong glance at Cat told her the conversation was far from over.

"Which one?" Another Whopper down the hatch. Cat seemed to have inherited her father's metabolism. She could eat cosmic crap tons of whatever the hell she wanted and she didn't gain an ounce. Bitch. "High school?"

Clare shook her head. Still red.

"College?"

Another head shake. If a kangaroo could hop across the intersection to change the topic of conversation from Elliott fucking Swift that would be great. Perhaps answering the question and giving her something, anything to mull over, would shut up the inquisition.

"Kindergarten." There. She'd given her something to chew on. It wasn't exactly a salacious detail, but it was something.

Cat coughed, choking on a piece of candy, and thumped her chest a few times. "You've known him since you were little and you still acted like..." She waved her hand as though that was enough of an explanation of her behavior. She wasn't wrong.

Mercifully, the light changed to green, Clare let her foot off the brake, and a silence descended over the car. "Yeah."

After a few minutes Cat leaned forward and turned the radio on. "Mom?"

"Yeah?"

"What's his name?"

"Elliott."

"I gave him your number."

CHAPTER 2
Clare

Clare's heart thrashed in her chest the whole way home as she fought the tug of her mind into memories of a long distant—but never forgotten—past. Catriona had given Elliott her number, so what?

If he really wanted it, he could have asked his parents for it. They were still friends with her parents and she'd seen them a handful of times throughout the years. Maybe he even still had it in his own cell phone. It wasn't like she'd changed it in the decades they'd known each other. Her stomach flipped. What if he'd deleted it? Ugh. The idea made her feel even more pathetic.

Had she kept her cell number in the hopes that he'd come back from becoming a hot-shot-hockey-player and want to talk to her all those years ago? Perhaps.

She'd need to come up with something particularly grueling to punish Cat for overstepping her bounds. She might have had one foot out the door toward college life, but as long as she stayed under Clare's—albeit falling down in places—roof, she was at Clare's mercy.

Maybe she'd make her clean the toilets with a toothbrush.

Or babysit for her little brother for a few nights without pay. Or—

"Mom?" Mason's voice startled her from her revenge plotting.

"Yeah, honey?"

"Are you okay?"

"Sure, baby. I'm good. Why do you ask?"

He pointed at the still running faucet. "You've been washing that carrot for about four minutes now. I think it's clean."

Turning off the water, she smiled and dried off her hands, placing the carrot on the counter next to the rest of the vegetables. "I guess I'm just a little distracted." She ruffled his hair.

His eyes narrowed, but he shrugged and his stomach growled. "How long till dinner?"

"About twenty minutes."

Another nod and he took off through the house before she could follow it up, so she yelled.

"Put your laundry away before screens, Masemallow. It's on your bed." She slid the knife through the head of broccoli, collected the florets in cupped hands and put them into a bowl. "Mase?" She paused to wait for a reply.

"I got it. I got it. Laundry before games."

"Distracted by Dishy Elliot?" Catriona crossed the kitchen, reached around Clare, and swiped a piece of carrot.

"Eavesdropping?"

"Always. Tell me how you met him."

Clare sighed. Elliot was exactly what she was distracted by. Seeing him again had pulled the dusty old cover off the box of long-forgotten feels in her chest. Now that it had been uncovered, it was growing, sucking the air from her body and demanding attention. "I met him on the first day of kindergarten. I told you."

"Okay? Is that it? You guys...just...went to school together like two strangers?"

No. "Yup."

"Funny. I didn't get a strangers vibe. I got scandalous history vibe. You want me to believe you just met on the first day of school and that's the end of your story?" She narrowed her gaze and folded her arms. Audacious sass filled the kitchen, and Cat wore an incredulous look that Clare herself had perfected over the years. Though Clare's eyebrows weren't anywhere near as flawless as her daughters.

"Yup." Dammit, she popped the 'p' too hard, made it too casual, brushed it off too quickly. Cat wasn't going to buy it. She needed to play it cool, act natural, maybe she wouldn't—

"Liar."

Some days she hated how well her oldest child knew her. "If I tell you how we met will you leave me alone to finish dinner?"

Cat waved the half-eaten stick of carrot at her. "We both know I can't promise that, Mom. But I can promise to help clean up after dinner."

"You help clean up after dinner every evening."

Cat bumped her hip against Clare's. "And I do such a swell job of it, too. You'll miss me when I'm on campus."

Her stomach soured. Cat was right—she was going to miss having her around. Sure, she'd still be in the same city, only a phone call away and able to see her regularly enough to save Clare from losing her fucking mind, but it stung.

"Spill, Mom. It's obviously weighing on your mind. Maybe it'll be good to get it off your chest."

She put down the knife and wiped her palms on the front of her shirt. Turning to face her daughter, she folded her arms. Maybe if she protected her chest, her duct-taped heart wouldn't threaten to break all over again.

"The first time I saw Elliott Swift, I walked right up to him and kicked him."

Catriona's mouth dropped open. "You're kidding."

She laughed. "I'm not. I charged right up to him in the playground, kicked his shin, and announced he was my boyfriend."

Cat's eyes widened. "Mom! That's... Wow. Aggressive much?" She waved a hand. "Continue."

"Continue what? That's it. That's how we met."

"And did this boy accept your violent and deranged relationship proposal?"

She turned back to the counter and tossed the veggies into the steamer. "He kicked me right back and said 'fine.' Of course, because he kicked me, I didn't want him anymore. And there ended the shortest relationship in the history of the world."

Catriona laughed so hard tears appeared in the corners of her eyes. "Did you cry?"

"Uh-huh. Squealed like a piggy until he clapped his hand over my mouth because he didn't want to hear me wailing anymore."

Cat laughed even harder, turning her back to the charcoal grey granite countertop while gripping the edge with both hands. "They don't write romance like that anymore."

"Right? Tale as old as motherfuckin' time."

"Were you mortal enemies from that moment on?"

"Best friends."

Cat shook her head. "You know, psychologists would have a field day with this." She paused, falling silent for a moment.

It was one of Clare's earliest memories, a core memory, something that made her warm and gooey inside. The day she'd met Elliott Swift was the day she'd been convinced she'd met her soul mate, even at only five years old. She knew.

She still knew.

And the pain at having lost him was so stifling, so unbearable, she had to find a way to shrink it back into its former space in her heart before it consumed her.

"What went wrong?"

"Oh, y'know..." She shrugged. "We grew up, we grew apart..." *He ran off and left me and never looked back.*

"You had me." A severe 'v' appeared between Cat's brows. While Mason was every bit of Clare poured into a little person —blue eyes and mousy brown straight hair—Catriona was a daily reminder of her chicken shit high school love who left her barefoot and pregnant. Not Elliott. Unfortunately for Clare she'd known a multitude of chicken shits in high school, and she'd given her virginity to one of them—Catriona's father, Ashton.

Sleek dark waves fell over her pale shoulders, and the most stunning bright green eyes she'd ever seen stared accusingly back at her. Like Elliott leaving to play hockey, Ashton had never looked back, either.

There was no mistaking her daughter's beauty, which mercifully hadn't yet been an issue as she was more interested in getting into a good college and keeping her grades up than going out to parties or dating. Books, not boys. That had been her motto since she'd discovered a love of astronomy and classic literature at an early age.

It wouldn't last forever, and Clare was already prepared to do hard time for slaying the first boy who broke her girl's beautiful heart.

Cupping Cat's chin with both her hands, she dropped a kiss on her forehead. "Yeah, KitKat. I had you. But that's not what pulled us apart. Our friendship was already broken by the time I got pregnant with you."

A wave of bone-deep sadness threatened to drag her under. She gave Cat a watery smile, swallowed down the shards of agony lodged in her throat, and patted her cheek. "Everything happens for a reason, right?"

Cat worked her bottom lip with her teeth. "What did he do to you, Mom?"

She stepped back and gestured to the silverware drawer. "Set the table for dinner, please."

Cat didn't move. "Mom?"

She sighed. "He left, baby girl. He went off to play hockey and never looked back. I guess when he returned and found out I had you and was a single mom... Maybe he was hurt, maybe he was angry, maybe..." She dropped her hands to her sides with a frustrated sigh. "I dunno. It would have been too much for any young adult to come home to."

It had been too much for Cat's father. He had wanted Clare to get an abortion, and when she had refused, he walked. He was with a new girlfriend less than a month later, and made sure that their entire freakin' class knew why they were no longer together. Word of her being knocked up had spread like wildfire, and she didn't even have her best friend by her side to stem the tide of the inherent meanness that came with the teenage years.

"Maybe it was something else." Cat sprang into action, pulling silverware from the drawer and placing it on the table.

She frowned and tipped her head. "Like what?"

It was Cat's turn to shrug. "I dunno. But maybe something stopped him from coming back to you. Maybe your meeting in the feminine hygiene aisle of CVS was the universe's way of telling you to get your head out of your ass and go talk to the man."

She smacked Clare's butt. "You deserve to be happy, Mom. Just because he-who-won't-be-named...okay, *two* asshats...fine, *they*-who-won't-be-named made you feel undeserving, doesn't mean that *you* are undeserving."

"Since when are you so smart?"

"Since I had a great mom who taught me about self-worth from an early age. It's hard to see you so down on yourself like this, Mom. I saw how Elliott looked at you in the store... How you looked at him... There was something there. And sure, it might not be a forever thing, but isn't it worth a look? It could be."

"You've been reading romance novels again, haven't you?"

"*Wuthering Heights*. Fucking love me some Heathcliff. Cathy needed a slap." Catriona released a dreamy sigh. "What can I say, Mom? There's something magical about reading about two people falling in love. I just think there's a reason you bumped into him in the tampon aisle of all places, and you shouldn't dismiss it just because you're upset at him for something he did twenty years ago."

Another shrug. "Even if it was something shitty. Really shitty. It's important to forgive, Mom. You taught me that, too." She flicked her eyes to the ceiling like she had all the answers to the world's problems and Clare was an idiot. She even said it like Clare would have if the roles were reversed. Ugh. She was getting her own advice back at her from her spirited nineteen-year-old.

While she didn't want to admit her child was right—she couldn't stand the smugness or gloating—she was certainly right about one thing: he was in the tampon aisle. Tampons meant a wife, girlfriend, or daughter. Her heart sank. Even if she could get herself past the distress curdling her stomach, there was every chance he was already with someone.

Cat pointed at Clare's face. "I see what you're doing, Mom. Christ, your brain is so loud sometimes."

"Okay, smartass, what am I doing?"

"You're telling yourself you're not good enough for him somehow, or that he already has someone. Well, get that out of your head right now. He doesn't. I checked."

Her stomach dropped to her feet as a wave of nausea

crashed over her. "You asked him if he was *married*? How much did you talk to the man?" Cat was like Clare in some ways—when she wasn't stunned into embarrassment and flustered silence anyway, she could certainly talk.

Cat snorted. "More than you managed to. But, no. I didn't ask him if he was married. He had no ring, no band of white skin around his finger where a ring might have been, and he didn't pick up any of the products in that aisle."

"Okay, Sherlock Holmes. Some people never wear their wedding band. No ring doesn't mean no partner."

Catriona rolled her eyes. Clare would have to start charging her a buck for every time she did it—she'd be able to cover the cost of her entire college tuition within a month.

"You could just say Sherlock, Mom. I know who he is. You don't need the Holmes. And I know that."

The oven timer chimed, and Cat tossed the oven mitts lying next to her at Clare. "I just feel in my bones that he's single though."

Oh, to have the confidence of a helpless romantic who hadn't yet been jaded by the world around her.

"Well, no offense, kiddo. But I don't really put much stock in your bones when it comes to matters of the heart." She slipped on an oven mitt and jerked open the oven, stepping to the side to avoid the gust of hot air. She eased the bubbling hotdish out and onto a trivet in the middle of the table.

Cat gasped and clutched her chest. "I'm wounded, Mom. Wounded. But when things work out between you and that dreamboat, I'm not going to be shy about telling you I told you so."

"Dreamboat?"

Cat had already slipped onto a chair and was scooping a heaped portion of food onto her plate. "I won't let you deflect by poking fun at my choice of vocabulary. But I also have a date burning the roof of my mouth with molten lava cheese so we're going to have to circle back."

She jabbed her fork into the mound of food and blew on the steaming bite. "You probably still have his number, don't you? You could totally text him first. You are a modern woman after all." She wiggled her eyebrows before eating the food. "Mmm! So freakin' good, Mom."

"Apparently, in all my years of teaching, I didn't get around to dinner etiquette. Mason! Come eat before your rude sissy eats it all."

"I can't help it. Expecting me not to demolish this deliciousness" —she waved her hand at the casserole dish— "as soon as it comes out of the oven… It's just cruel and unusual."

Clare chuckled as she got the veggies out of the steamer and put them into a serving dish.

"Dad wants to know if you can change weekends with him. He's got something this weekend so he said he can take me next weekend." Mason tugged open the fridge and grabbed the gallon container of chocolate milk, followed by a glass from the cabinet next to the sink.

From the moment they had separated, Captain Asshole had used Mason as a method of communication. As her grandma used to say, it boiled her piss. Why couldn't he simply pick up the phone and drop her a text like any normal grown-ass adult instead of using their child to pass messages to her?

To Mason though, his dad hung the moon in the sky and rearranged the stars just for funsies. He probably thought he created the planets, too.

"I'll text him, Mase. Eat." She motioned to his empty plate with the dish of veggies in her hand.

She never gave an answer back to Mason, always replied to his dad's game of telephone through text so there was a record of everything right there in her trusty cell phone chat history.

That way, Commander Douche Nozzle couldn't re-write his own version of the truth and nothing could come back to bite her in the ass. Theoretically, anyway.

Ugh. It had been so long since she'd been bitten *anywhere*. Clearing her throat, she brushed away lusty thoughts of Elliott biting her ass cheek. Or at least tried to. Once she let it into her mind there was no escaping the fact she'd pretty much let Elliott bite her anywhere.

"Mom?" Cat speared her with a look, fork paused midway between the table and her mouth. "Sit. Eat. Texting *him* back can wait."

Schooling her face, Clare took her seat. Cat was too perceptive for her own damn good. Thankfully, she must have her *I hate my ex-husband* face on again rather than her *I wanna do naughty things to my childhood sweetheart* face.

What could life have been like if Elliott had come back from hockey instead of staying away?

Nope. She wouldn't let herself fall down that rabbit hole. Her path had given her two perfect, beautiful children that she never once regretted even if their fathers were both complete jerks. Though Elliott had left her too, ergo—also a jerk.

She needed to put those beautiful eyes and that lopsided smile out of her mind, and panties, forever. Nothing good could come of opening the door to their past. It was behind them. Despite living in the same city, Mason playing hockey, and Elliott coaching the college kids, she'd managed to avoid bumping into him for almost two decades. With any luck, she wouldn't see him again for another two.

CHAPTER 3
Elliott

Even though the junior high-aged team was training on the ice pad, Elliott sat in the stands surrounded by loose pages and highlighters. Something about the cool, crisp air in the rink and the sound of skates cutting through ice, no matter who was skating, made it easier for him to think.

Down below, the AAA team finished their warm up and were breaking out into small groups to work on their puck handling and skills. Like putting together a championship winning team wasn't hard enough, rebuilding when star players graduated college and stepped out into the big bad world all by themselves felt unachievable some years.

Coach of the AAA team, Will Morrison, had been the best damn captain the Snow Pirates had seen for as long as Elliott had been the coach, and filling the kid's shoes...well, it felt kind of impossible. Picking up the print out of the roster, he studied his team's stats again. He could probably recite them in his sleep.

Every season it was as though the details of his players were tattooed onto the insides of his eyelids. He knew them better than he knew himself. Their strengths, their weaknesses, their women, their superstitions. He knew it all. And he also knew that it always took a little time for things to settle and the guys to find their flow, but this season felt insurmountable given what had gone before.

It didn't help that his ex-wife Denise was busting his balls yet again. You'd think considering the fact they had no kids, they didn't work together or live together, that she already had someone new, *and* she'd gotten everything in the fucking divorce would mean that she had no business anywhere near him. But you'd be wrong.

It would seem he had been a serial killer in a previous life, being punished with the most unrelenting, manipulative pain in the ass woman to ever walk the face of the earth.

Like it wasn't bad enough she'd gotten the house and all their shit, while he got all the goddamned bills, but she still called him when the faucet was leaking, or she had a fight with her boyfriend. She drunk dialed Elliott in the middle of the night to regale him with their good ole days. While he struggled to recall any good ole days at all.

With a frustrated sigh, he slammed the pages onto his thighs before collecting them into a semi-tidy pile and tucking them under his arm. Maybe working at the rink wasn't what he needed today. He stood up and descended the steps down to the boards to watch the maneuvers on the ice for a few minutes before leaving.

The thirteen- and fourteen-year-olds were his favorite to watch play. Hungry, determined, and not quite old enough to know how good they were or let their egos get in the way of just playing some damn good hockey.

The ice was split at the top of the circles for two-on-one drills. The play area was cut in half so two smaller drill teams could work side by side. It was a fun exercise he loved to use for his own team, and one that worked on moving, thinking, being creative and some decision making thrown in there for good measure, too. A great all-round drill to see what skills the kids on the ice actually had.

The puck was dumped in the middle, forcing the players to work hard to get it to their side and create a two-on-one situation. At that point, the team who *didn't* win the puck had the opportunity to make it a three-on-one, or a three-on-two if they wanted by crossing the middle line and joining the guys who had won possession.

As the drill unfolded, one of the forwards remained in his zone while his teammates made a three-on-two situation in the other side of the ice. The rule was he could be anywhere within his space—a high-risk, high-reward ploy, leaving him by himself as his teammates pursued the puck in the other zone.

Whoever the kid was needed to bend his knees and move his stick a little more, but he smacked his blade on the ice, calling for the biscuit as his linemate picked up the puck and sailed it back into their area to his waiting stick. He glanced up at the net, didn't hesitate, took a swing and scored.

Nice.

Their coach—Will Morrison—, was busy explaining something to the defenseman on the other team so Elliott decided to bestow a little wisdom on the boy.

"Hey, kid."

Three kids glanced his way, but none of them was the one he wanted. He pointed at number six, and his teammate tapped his stick on his shin before pointing it towards Elliott at the edge of the rink.

Elliott jerked his head in a *c'mere* motion.

As the kid skated, he removed his helmet and jammed it under his elbow. "Yeah, Coach?"

Elliott was surprised by his response. Most of the young teens on the ice wouldn't have had the first clue who he was yet. "Nice play. Patience is important out there, and you stayed aware of the puck despite the fact it probably wouldn't have come back to you."

He was saying things the kid already knew, but he liked to start his feedback with the good stuff. That way his players knew there were things about their game that were solid before he got to what they could improve on.

"Bend your knees a little more, it'll help."

The kid nodded like he'd been told that a thousand times.

"And keep that stick active."

That one seemed to give him pause and his brows crashed together in a frown.

From center ice, Morrison yelled, "Run it again." And the players reset.

"Thanks, Coach." The kid skated away from him and back to position.

Something about him was familiar, but Elliott couldn't figure out what. When he got home he was going to Google some ways to help the kid bend his knees more. It had been years since he'd taught anyone below college level. He was rusty, but as good as Will was, coaching the minor teams was his first coaching gig, and he would probably be glad for the assist.

"Coach." Morrison came to a stop next to the boards Elliott was leaning on. "How're things?"

"Oh, you know." He shrugged. "Same old. Trying to put together a championship team when some of our best players grew up and moved on."

Will smiled. "It's funny, because when you're out there on the ice, none of us ever feel like we're the best players. We're just cogs in the team machine, Coach. Doing our part to bring the team to glory."

"Repeating my words back to me, eh?" He brushed his palm along his jaw. "Kid's good." He jerked his chin to the player he'd been talking to.

"Mason? He is. Still can't get him to bend those knees quite right, but he's got potential." Will nodded. "They all do. I just need to figure out how to tap into that and bring it out of them. Like you did." He elbowed Elliott. "Gotta get them ready for their bright future with the Snow Pirates."

"Is it okay for me to watch for a bit? Helps my thought process."

Will grinned. "All your secrets are coming out now, Coach. I had no idea how complex your method is. We all just figured you woke up and shit greatness."

If only it were that simple. The pressure to succeed—especially after having delivered a championship season—was stifling. It was never enough. There were always better players, new objectives, teams to beat and another cup to win.

For the next thirty minutes, Elliott strategized plays and drills to the background music of teenagers yelling and skating. When their practice ended, he figured it was time for him to head out also.

And finally he realized why Mason seemed familiar.

Clare stood next to a beat-up white Camry in the parking lot with her hands planted on her hips and her face stern as she stared down at the kid who had her eyes. She wore a black graphic t-shirt that said *I'm too clumsy to be around fragile masculinity*, a long yellow cardigan and dark wash jeans with black ankle boots.

Her lips were pursed and her eyes narrowed. He'd seen that look a million times before—hell, he'd been on the receiving end of it more times than he cared to remember. He turned his head in case she saw him grinning at the memory.

"But Mooooooom." Mason's whining carried through the air as Elliott made his way to his SUV. "Dad said—"

She practically snarled. "Mason, I've talked to you before about playing your father and me off of one another. You knew I wouldn't be happy about it and you did it anyway. I'll be talking to your dad when we get home."

Elliott winced. Clare's daughter hadn't mentioned that Clare was with someone when she'd given him her number. Maybe she thought her mom needed to connect with an old friend. Maybe Elliott had just hoped to find her unattached.

But Clare had another kid and was still with their father. Of course she was. Any guy who gave her up would be dumb as a bag of rocks. But until he'd heard her mention Mason's father, he hadn't realized how much he'd hoped to find her single. If he'd been a better man and committed to her all those years ago, he'd never have given her up either.

Guilt swirled in his sour stomach as he watched the exchange between the two. She was married, taken, unavailable, but his heart—and his dick—didn't seem to be understanding that meant a big old "nope" was painted across the entire situation like caution tape at a crime scene.

He remembered how soft her skin was as he'd brush her wispy, dirty blond hair behind her ear. How plump her lips were, always shiny from the clear gloss she wore daily as a teenager. How stubborn she could be, how fiercely determined to accomplish anything she damn well wanted to without hesitation or self-doubt.

But he also remembered the betrayal in her eyes when he told her he had to go back on their deal and leave to play hockey. He remembered the sadness in her voice as she pleaded with him not to go and the tears as they trickled down her flushed cheeks as he walked away.

He pressed against his sternum with a clenched fist, but the welling pain wouldn't abate. She was married, with kids, happy, albeit a little disheveled and somewhat odd but that was always who she was.

He couldn't have her. He'd missed his chance. She was in

his past. There was no future for them. It did no good to stew over roads not taken.

As he crossed the parking lot, he heard a gear bag fall to the ground and turned in time to see Mason storming away from Clare. Elliott beeped open his SUV with the key fob but didn't take his eyes off her.

Anguish paled her delicate features as she chewed on her thumbnail. She covered her face with both palms and stood, shoulders curled forward and bobbing with what had to be quiet sobs. He wanted to go to her, to wrap his arms around her and tell her it would all be okay. But he couldn't.

He never had kids with Denise, though there was a time he'd have given anything to have them. She kept putting him off and putting him off until she finally confessed she had never actually wanted kids at all. It had been the beginning of the end for them.

Married under the pretense of wanting the same things out of life left only mistrust and heartache when the truth came out, and a marriage built on mistrust was no marriage at all.

He rubbed his chest again. So many things he could have and should have done differently over the years. He'd come home ready to settle down with Clare only to find her pregnant with another man's kid. When he'd met Denise he thought he could maybe be happy with her, until it came out that she'd lied about wanting kids. The kicker came when she stepped out on their marriage with her boss.

He grunted. Clearly his instincts couldn't be trusted. Women couldn't be trusted.

The unexpected trip down memory lane was giving him indigestion and the bitter taste of betrayal coated the back of his tongue. He needed to get in his car and leave, to go home, throw some leftovers into the microwave and watch some game tapes to see if he could figure out how to fill the shoes of the hockey giants who'd left his team.

If that was truly what he needed, then why could he not urge his feet to move until Clare had pulled herself together and driven after Mason?

In the driver's seat of his car in the empty parking lot, he picked up his phone and hovered his thumb over her name in his contacts. His brain condemned the idea entirely, but his heart spurred him forward. Sure, she was out of bounds romantically, but they could be friends again, right? She certainly looked like she could use a friend. And what could be the harm in sending her a message telling her it was nice to see her?

Elliott had been gone from Minnesota for a year, playing hockey and traveling the country. But he was back—albeit temporarily—and he wanted to see his girl. Just thinking about Clare loosened the straps around his chest.

He'd missed her. So fucking much.

He'd missed her seventeenth birthday, the Fourth of July, Halloween, Thanksgiving, and Christmas—all their favorite holidays. He'd missed it all. Had she done everything they used to do, but with someone else?

They had so much to catch up on. What they'd been doing, how things were going, and they sure as hell needed to talk.

Christ, did they ever need to talk.

She worked in a small, family-owned frozen yogurt place after school and on the weekends. Her parents had told him what shift she was on so he could surprise her, and when he hopped off the bus and tossed his equipment bag in the trunk of his parent's car, butterflies warred in his stomach.

Would she have forgiven him for leaving? Maybe. But probably not.

Clare Reynolds could hold a grudge better than anyone else he'd ever met. Sure, he'd hurt her by going to play hockey, and the look of soul-deep betrayal on her face when he'd left was forever burned into his memory. But hopefully her love for him, for their friendship, their history together, would make her see reason and forgive him for chasing his dream across the country.

She hadn't broken her radio silence and called him, nor had she answered any of his ten thousand—okay that might have been a slight exaggeration, but it didn't feel like it—messages. But now he was back in town and going to stand in front of her —she couldn't ignore that.

Well, she could try, but he wouldn't let her. She meant too much to him not to fight for her. And he was going to fight with all he had.

He'd tell her that, too. That he loved her. That he'd always loved her. He'd fought it at first, then feared it, then as their friendship grew, so did his fear of fucking everything up by telling her he had more-than-friend feelings for her.

But he wasn't afraid anymore. He missed her. Every single fucking day he was away from Minnesota left deep gashes on his soul and he was going to tell her. He was going to kiss her until she stopped being mad at him, and for backup, he was going to bring her peonies as a peace offering—she fucking loved peonies.

He had a plan, he had a bouquet of fragrant peonies on the passenger seat next to him, and a nausea so fierce he almost changed his mind and drove home for Mom's meatloaf. But he needed to tell her how he felt, even if she hated him.

If she hit him, he'd take it like the hockey player he was. Then he'd kiss the fight right out of her.

Creamy Dreams was bustling. They had a killer two-for-one deal on Thursday nights that brought damn near everyone in the city to their doors. He squeezed through the tightly packed bodies clumped around the entrance and scanned behind the counter.

Her back was to him as he stood against the far wall, peeking between customers to steal a glimpse of her, but he could pick out that mousy brown, messy bun anywhere. When she turned, she took his breath away, flushed pink cheeks, bright red lips and a matching red bow tied around her bun.

She pressed the heel of her hand to her temple and blew air upwards, making her bangs flop against her forehead. It was hot as Hades in the small store. She wore a lime green polo shirt that seemed snug fitting around her tits.

Holy shit, she'd filled out.

She took a step away from the counter, pushed her hand into the small of her back and arched her body, bringing the rest of her torso into view. Was that a...bump? He stopped breathing. Stared dumbfounded at the woman he loved more than life itself.

She was pregnant? Why hadn't his parents told him she was with someone? Prepared him for the fact he was going to show up to win her back by telling him to expect to find her ready to pop out a fucking kid. Why hadn't they saved him from the soul-tearing agony and embarrassment crawling all over his body at the sight?

But he couldn't look away. She was an incredibly stunning mother—though he wasn't sure whether the glow was from the overhead lights, the temperature of the room, or the fact that she was so beautifully pregnant.

Either way, she was the most breathtaking vision in a lime green polo shirt he'd ever seen. But she was someone else's now. He'd lost her for real and there was nothing he could say or do to get her back. And even if there was, he wasn't the kind of man to break up a relationship for his own benefit.

Fuck.

Backing out through the crowd, he was careful not to be seen.

On the sidewalk outside, an elderly woman ate froyo at a table. When she met his gaze, he handed her the flowers without a word, and trudged back to his car.

Every step away from Clare hurt more than the last, and by the time he closed the car door and started the ignition, the pain was so deep, so acute, that he was sure he would die on the spot.

How could this have happened? How could she have moved on from him so quickly? Every day he'd been missing her, pining for her, and she'd been sleeping with someone new.

Bile rose in his throat as he gripped the steering wheel with white knuckles. Sparks of anger and betrayal flared inside his chest and blazed through his pain. He was pissed. Pissed at her for not answering his texts, pissed at her for holding his dream against him, pissed at her for finding someone new, for getting pregnant, for not telling him…

But most of all he was pissed at himself for losing the one thing he cherished the most. He'd lived without her in his world for a year and it had been too much. How could he face the rest of his life without her?

CHAPTER 4
Clare

"Mozzarella sticks?"

Clare lifted her hand to indicate to the bartender the sticks were hers. If he gave away her fried cheese to someone else, she'd be forced to cause bodily harm. She'd do damn near anything for good mozzarella sticks. Apparently that included attacking a bartender.

"Thank you." She offered a grateful smile as he placed the red basket in front of her.

"Sure. You want another?" He gestured at her almost empty glass and she nodded.

He crushed up fresh raspberries and squeezed them through a cloth bag to strain the juice, added Limoncello, vodka, and a simple sugar syrup before topping it off with Sprite Zero. As delicious as the cocktail was, he was pretty delish himself, and his delectable biceps flexed as he worked.

He was more muscular than she'd normally go for, and younger, probably too young in fact, but when it had been... Well, far too long since she'd felt the intimate touch of another human being. Beggars couldn't be choosers.

He sucked his teeth as he handed her the glass. A reminder of just how comfortable she'd gotten being alone. Sucking your teeth wasn't a crime, hell, it wasn't even the worst of the bad habits a person could have. But the mere action made her want to grab him by the ear and twist like her mama used to do any time she caught her biting her nails as a child.

She thanked him and turned back to her book boyfriend. The men between the covers of a romance novel didn't let you down. Or rather, they let you down all the time, but they also usually distracted you with washboard abs and exceedingly large penises that they all magically knew what to do with, giving their heroines screaming back-to-back orgasms at the drop of a hat.

She smirked. Nothing quite brought her stress levels down like a good smutty book. She turned the page. *Praise,* by Sara Cate wasn't something she'd usually pick up. But Cat had read it and *raved* about it.

At first she'd thought it was odd—perhaps even a little icky—that her almost-not-a-teenager-anymore was recommending filthy books to her, but she kind of liked it. Clare didn't have a lot of free time, and whatever spare time she had, she didn't want to spend it reading terrible books.

Cat was her willing pre-screener, and since she started taking her daughter's recommendations, she hadn't read a single book she wasn't obsessed with. Her list of book boyfriends was growing week by week.

A loud tut pulled her attention from Charlotte and Emerson. A woman stood, leaning over the bar, a twenty clutched in her perfectly manicured hand. Clare focused on her book again, assuming the tut was one of impatience, and the woman wasn't thrilled about having to wait a whole thirty seconds for service. But instead, the lady stared at her.

"Aren't you embarrassed to be seen with...that?"

Clare turned her attention back to the tutter. "Excuse me?"

"Aren't you embarrassed to be reading smut in public?"

Clare snorted. "You think this is bad?" She waved the book at the stranger. As romance novel covers went it was mild. Sure, the guy on it was hot AF and had his shirt open a bit, but at least he was *wearing* a shirt. It was only a semi man-chest rather than full frontal and his V leading to the Promised Land of Peen wasn't even showing.

"Ha! You should be glad I didn't bring any of my sports romance novels along tonight." She dropped her voice like she was sharing salacious gossip. "The models on those ones don't have a shirt on at all." She gasped theatrically and clutched at her chest. "Scandalous."

The bartender leaned across the bar. "I really liked that one." He winked at Clare.

"Y-you've read that?" The woman's jaw would dislocate if it hung open much more.

Clare hid a grin behind the pages of her book.

"I have. I totally think more men should read romance novels. I love anything that's spicy as all get out, and if it has voyeurism in it..." He whistled. "And who doesn't love a praise kink?"

He fanned his face with an open hand. "My husband and I take turns reading chapters to each other every night before bed. Keeps things fresh in the boudoir, you know?" He spoke to Clare like they were old friends.

Ugh. He read romance novels and spoke smut. It was a home run. But strike one for the teeth sucking. Strike two for the fact he was gay. Strike three for the fact he had a husband. She'd have to find someone else to fantasize about.

"My daughter loved it and said I needed to read it, so here I am."

"But reading in a bar by yourself. Isn't that a little...pathetic?" Tutter cringed like the word tasted gross in her mouth.

Bitterness bubbled at the back of Clare's throat and she opened her mouth to respond, not really sure what she'd say. She *felt* pathetic, more so now she'd been called out on it for sure. But if she didn't venture out into the world to sit among other grown adults—even somewhere like a bustling bar where she didn't even talk to anyone but the bartender—she'd spend her whole life hiding alone in her house. Wouldn't that be more pathetic?

"Personally, I think it's pathetic that a grown-ass woman can't keep her acerbic opinions to herself." Her new bartender friend flashed a movie-ready smile.

The stranger gasped.

"One thing I hate most when I'm reading a book? Being interrupted. It's like, dude, my nose is literally between the pages and I'm in another world. But being interrupted to be insulted? That's some next level bullshit."

Oh. She liked him. A lot.

The dressed down smut-hater rolled her lips between her teeth before mouthing thank you to the bartender, but she couldn't just let it the fuck go. "I just don't think it's appropriate to read trashy novels in a bar."

"As things go, it's nowhere near the worst I've seen in a bar. She's not reading it aloud. She's not beating you with the book. She's literally minding her own business and reading a freakin' book. In fact, until you came up to order a drink I'm sure she didn't even know you were there. This is most definitely a you problem, not a her problem."

The woman's face turned red, and she muttered to herself about romance novels being shameful and giving women a bad name. After she'd walked away with her glasses of wine, Clare thanked the man again and bit into a mozzarella stick.

He waved her off. "Anytime you want to talk smut, I'm

your guy. We're in a smutty book club too if you want the details."

"I'd like that."

She returned her attention to her paperback, but a boisterous group of well-dressed young men arrived in the bar all at once and her stomach dropped. Hockey players. Worse still, Snow Pirates. Elliott's Snow Pirates. As much as the coach generally didn't socialize with his team, it was another reminder of *him* that she didn't need.

She'd seen him twice since the pharmacy *incident*. Both times they'd remained cordial, pleasant, and he was a true gent who mentioned that she had half a Cheeto caught in her hair.

She had avoided him for twenty fucking years even though they lived in the same town. She had assumed CVS had been a weird coincidence, that the world would right itself and she wouldn't see him for another twenty years, but apparently, that wasn't to be.

He just kept showing up. And so did her decade's old feeling bubbling not-so-deep in her chest. Ugh.

She sighed and shoved another mozzarella stick in her mouth. Perhaps if she kept feeding her feelings fried cheese she would stop caring about the fact she'd seen Elliott again. Or maybe the cheese would kill her rage. Ha! Perhaps cheese was the cure for anger and no one had ever eaten enough to see the results.

Challenge accepted.

"This seat taken?"

She breathed and swallowed at the same time, the cheese lodged in the back of her mouth, and her eyes watered. She was not choking to death on a cheese stick in front of Elliott fucking Swift. No, sir-ee. That was not how her story ended. Not today, anyway.

She took a huge swig of her drink, hoping it would push down both the wad of cheese stuck in her esophagus and the mortification of him finding her alone in a bar, eating said cheese and reading smut.

"Clare?"

When she turned to face him she was almost touched by the concern wrinkling his brow.

"Is there anyone sitting here?"

Oh. Yes. He'd asked a question and was standing awkwardly, waiting for an invitation to sit. Oh God, he wanted to join her, maybe even to talk. She swallowed. How could she get out of it?

She couldn't talk to him, stare at him, sit near him because she'd want to *do* things to him, *with* him. Things like rake her teeth along his jaw, or run her fingers over every damn inch of him like he was hers to touch.

Dear God above, did she ever want to smell him?

Only a little sniff. Just to see if her memory of him was accurate. She could slide her fingers into the hair at his nape and tug so his head jerked back giving her space to smush her face into the side of his neck and breathe deep.

Yeah, she'd made it weird, and she needed to get the fuck out of there before she acted on the impulses brewing underneath her skin.

She could try to make up an imaginary friend, but the picture of her reading in a bar alone or chatting to the bartender didn't lend itself to her being with someone. Fall off her stool? Nope. He'd rush to her aid and make sure she got home safely.

Fuck sticks. She was trapped.

She pointed at the stool next to her with her book. "You can sit."

"Thanks." He asked the bartender for a Sam Adams and slid onto the seat beside her. Their biceps touched. Just a couple of inches of skin sitting close enough together to feel his warmth through her shirt, but it was enough.

Her body was in overdrive, urging her to act, to touch him, to yell at him, do…something. Anything. The desire to angry fuck him out of her system for doing her wrong all those years ago was overwhelming.

She downed her drink, and her new bestie behind the bar had collected the glass before she'd even put it down.

"I'll get you another." New Bestie side eyed Elliott like he knew there was something there. It would be hard not to. The history between them had gone from simmering to bubbling to boiling over, in fact.

It was tangible, like a living breathing thing that grew, consumed the space, suffocated her, squeezed all rational thought from her thrumming body.

She couldn't keep running into him and straying down memory lane. Never mind her broken heart—her throbbing girl parts couldn't take it.

"How're things?" He took a sip from his beer, and try as she might to keep her eyes off the way his lips wrapped around the bottle, she couldn't.

As soon as she got home she was ordering a new vibrator. She needed to get her stupid, double-crossing libido under control. God damn the bartender for being gay and married. Double ugh.

How were things? What a seemingly innocent question, but it was charged with intrigue. Should she tell him how things truly were? How she was a single mom on the wrong side of thirty, raising two teenagers, one of whom was about to flee the nest and go out on her own.

Should she tell him how she hated her life, her job, her exes, but mostly herself? How she couldn't meet her own eyes in the goddamn mirror every morning because she didn't recognize who she saw staring back at her anymore?

No. She couldn't go there. The book thing with the stranger was embarrassing enough. Clare didn't want

Elliott's pity, his sympathy, or worse—his advice on how to fix it.

He cleared his throat and took another drink of his beer.

Nope. She did not want his pity. But she sure as fuck wanted his mouth. Around her nipple. Strike that. On any part of her body. She wasn't fussy.

"Things are..." How to answer without lying? She might not have seen him in a long while, but she'd bet her bottom dollar that he still knew her every bit as well as he did all those years ago. "They're okay. My daughter, Cat, is staying at a friend's tonight, and my son, Mason, is at his dad's."

An almost imperceptible twitch of his eyebrow was the only reaction he gave as he took another mouthful. The bartender placed another drink in front of her and patted her hand twice.

He'd poured her a double. She was going to buy him a romance novel to thank him for being so freakin' perceptive. New Bestie was the real MVP.

She took a huge gulp of her drink, willing the alcohol to weave its way into her muscles and help her relax. Maybe she'd tell Elliott about her work. That was safe territory. There was nothing sexy or inviting about clerical duties.

"I'm a medical transcriptionist." She leveled him with a stare, almost daring him to say something derogatory about how she used to always want to be a doctor and now she was essentially a doctor's glorified secretary.

She winced. She wasn't. But some days that's sure as shit how it felt.

"When I got pregnant with Cat..." Clare swallowed, staring across the bar. She didn't owe him an explanation, and he wasn't pressing for them, but she needed to drown out the urge to grab him by his stupid collar and kiss his stupid face and she couldn't stop the word vomit. "College wasn't in the cards for me. I went to community college when Cat got a little older. Studied evenings and nap times." She gave an awkward laugh.

"Do you enjoy it?"

Did she? Not really. But she'd done it for so long she'd just accepted that it was a means to an end. Kids were expensive, clothes were expensive, food and utilities were expensive, car maintenance was expensive, college was going to be expensive, and as much as Mason's dad helped out, her job—while it didn't light her fire—was stable.

And she needed stable. Reliable. Secure. Not to mention, it provided decent health insurance—which didn't hurt when she had an accident prone kid who played a sport involving high speed projectiles and metal blades strapped to his feet.

"It pays the bills." She sighed, picking at the corner of her coaster. Her boss was up for promotion and she was salty as hell about it. He'd been the best supervisor she'd ever had. All the others had been asshole idiots, promoted beyond their abilities, or left for greener pastures.

She could have done their job in her sleep, and in a tiny part of her mind, she always wondered what it would have been like if she'd thrown her hat in the ring.

She could advance to a supervisory position, become a medical records and health information technician, medical coder, or medical records and health information administrator with additional education and training. Or leave the medical field altogether and do something else, something different, something fun.

There were options, she just hadn't taken them, or even considered them all that much. Her kids were her priority and her job was just that, a job, not a career. But the idea of breaking in another new boss weighed on her.

He pursed his lips but said nothing.

"What?"

"I just..." He shrugged and put the bottle down in front of

him. "The Clare I knew was vibrant, ballsy, afraid of nothing…"

The fucking nerve of this guy.

She held up a hand. "We haven't seen each other for twenty years, Elliott. Third hand information from my parents doesn't mean that you know me." She blew her hair out of her eyes.

"The Clare you knew wasn't a teenage mom who got knocked up at seventeen years old the first time she ever had sex. She wasn't pregnant, scared, and alone because the sperm donor hauled ass and left me to deal with the consequences of our actions when I wouldn't terminate." Wow. The conversation had gone from "Hey, long time, no see. Is this seat taken?" into deep and gnarly specifics really fucking quickly. She hadn't been prepared. She still wasn't prepared.

His nostrils flared as he tensed in his seat, but even if she wanted to stop the tirade pouring from her mouth, she couldn't. "She wasn't abandoned by her best friend." The slashes on her heart vibrated with such a deep ache she thought her chest might collapse in on itself. "The Clare you knew had dreams and hopes and goals to become a hot shot doctor so she could help people, make a difference in the world."

"The Clare you knew wasn't married to a complete asshole who had an affair for almost the entire time they were married. She wasn't a divorced mom of two, on the wrong side of thirty, who'd let herself go so much that her clothes no longer fit. And who'd lost herself to the point her only downtime was eating fried cheese and reading a smutty book in a bar on a Thursday evening."

Tears welled in her eyes, but she blinked them back, willing them not to fall. "So yeah. You're right. I'm doing a job I don't even enjoy anymore because it pays my bills. It'll help pay for Cat's college tuition and Mason's hockey equipment.

My boss is leaving. I'm more than qualified to replace him, and I just can't." Take that, asshat. She managed a ragged breath, though it didn't feel like any air got into her tight chest.

How could he possibly know that she wasn't "ballsy" any longer? Just because she worked a decent job didn't mean she wasn't sky-diving on the fucking weekends.

She shivered. Okay, fine. Nope. That would *never* happen. People should not jump out of perfectly good planes for no reason.

"Can't or won't?"

His words fanned the fire flickering in her gut. "Does it matter? I'll keep doing what I'm doing because it's what I have to do to provide for my family. A promotion would mean more work, longer hours, more responsibility, more stress." She ticked each reason off on her fingers. "It would affect my kids and I don't want that."

He lifted his hand and moved it toward her, she held her breath, but the contact never came. Instead, he slid his thumb up the neck of the bottle, leaving a trail through the condensation. Why wouldn't he touch her, goddammit?

His nostrils flared and a muscle in his cheek worked overtime as he sat in silence.

"For Christ's sake, Eli. Spit it out. Speak."

His hazel eyes flashed at her as his head snapped up.

"You've never been one to hold your tongue. If you have something to say, then say it." Clare took another drink, alcohol fueling her righteous indignation. Baiting him, goading him, taunting him had never worked well for her, but she couldn't help herself. She was jonesing for a fight and part of her wanted him to meet her there.

The alcohol was definitely kicking in, and his presence was affecting her in ways she couldn't resist and didn't like—except she loved it, and wanted to lean into it, but she couldn't. He'd left her and she couldn't trust him not to leave her again. Her kids deserved better. Hell, *she* deserved better.

"I might not know the full extent of what you've been through, Clare. But I can definitely relate to the cheating and the divorce." He gave her a bitter smile. "I know what it's like to feel lost and miserable. To feel alone. To feel like you're not good enough."

His hand rested on the bar, only inches from hers. She could close the gap, slide hers under his, maybe she could feel his warmth without getting lost in it, but she didn't.

"I might not have kids, but I like to think a part of me still knows you, Clare. Always giving. Always doing what's best for everyone else. But what about you, huh?" He took another drink, flexed his jaw, and stood.

Slipping his wallet out of his back pocket, he grunted as he flipped it open and dropped some bills on the bar.

"At some point, the kids will be grown and you'll be by yourself wondering how the hell you got there and grumbling about how you're too old to change it. Hell, you might even end up resenting them."

Folding his wallet back into his pocket, he sighed. "If I've learned anything from my failed marriage it's that pushing down all your own hopes and dreams for the sake of someone else isn't going to do any of you any good."

The pain etched across his face was like a punch to the solar plexus and the weight of his tone gave her pause. What had he put on hold for the sake of his ex-wife? Wait. He didn't have kids? Didn't he always want kids? Was that what he put on hold for his partner?

"Don't make yourself small, Clare. It's okay for you to not only want something more, but to pursue it with everything you are. Update your resume. Put yourself forward for the promotion, if for no other reason than to say that you can. That you did something just for yourself."

She hadn't updated her resume in... Well, she didn't even know how long. Did she even have one? What would she even update it with?

Can entertain a six year old while helping a teenager with her math homework?

Always has snacks and BandAids on hand?

Can stack coupons like a freakin' coupon queen?

Always knows the kid friendly places to eat and the cheapest places to have family fun?

That wasn't quite what they were going for.

"I can see your mind working. Always coming up with your shortcomings, never seeing what you're capable of, what you could be capable of if you just got the fuck out of your own stubborn way."

She folded her arms. He was getting a little too close for comfort with his character assassination of her. "Did you take your own advice, Mr. Know It All? Is that why you're not married anymore and kicking ass and taking names with a championship winning hockey team?"

At his infuriating brow quirk, she kept going. "Uh huh. I know things, too. It's not that easy for me, Elliott. I can't just decide one night in a bar while tipsy on Fizzy Kisses to change my whole life."

Okay, next time she was going to go off on a rant she'd make sure she picked something with a less ridiculous name than a Fizzy Kiss.

"The old Clare wouldn't think twice about it."

"Gah! Old Clare is *gone*. There remains only this haggard, chubby, saggy boobed worker bee who still loves fried cheese more than she should."

"Stop being afraid of what could go wrong. What about what could go right?"

The Band-Aid over their long distant past had snapped like an elastic band. They were no longer two people who used to know each other. Nope. They were all-the-way-in-deep like no time at all had passed and like they were the same people, just twenty years later.

She tipped her chin. She hadn't missed this. His smug, superior, *do as I say not as I do* attitude. He didn't know shit about her, her kids, or her life. What gave him the right to just swan back into her life after so long and give her commentary on it?

Except...he also wasn't wrong.

"You want some help updating your resume?"

Yes, please. "Thanks, but I can handle it myself. I've done just fine without your help for two decades thanks." Ouch. She winced. That was... Oof. Too far. Target acquired. Shots fired. Direct hit. Direct. Fucking. Hit. Eesh.

He looked like she'd kicked his puppy. "Okay. Well, you know where I am if you change your mind." He nodded to the bartender and turned to his players still huddled at the end of the bar.

He'd left way too much money for his beer.

"Eli?"

He paused and stepped back toward her. She lifted the cash from the counter. "You left too much."

"You know, it's so weird hearing my given name. My folks call me Son, my team and colleagues call me Coach, my ex calls me Satan... I almost forgot I had an actual name." His warm smile undid her.

She held out the cash, he took it, and handed it over to her new bestie. "That should cover her tab, too."

When she started to protest he put a finger over her lips. "It's the least I can do." He flinched, hesitated like he had something else to say, but then he was gone.

New Bestie whistled, leaning forward, his forearms on the edge of the bar. "You wanna talk about *that*?"

"There isn't enough fried cheese or Fizzy Kisses in all the world to make me talk about *that*."

"Boy's got it bad." He arched an eyebrow.

She snorted. "Guilt money." She shrugged and swallowed the last of her drink. "I won't ever say no to Fizzy Kisses and mozzarella sticks though. I'm not picky when it comes to snacks. A total snack ho."

"So noted. You sure you don't need to unload?"

She gave a sidelong glance at Elliott's back as he patted a player on the shoulder and made his way to the exit. She was drowning in the past, in her feelings, in sadness at what could have been and what never was. She had no idea what the hell she needed.

CHAPTER 5
Clare

When the doorbell rang, Clare almost rolled face-first off the couch. She hadn't ordered dinner yet, her kids weren't home, and she had already received the embarrassing pile of Amazon packages she'd ordered a few nights ago while under the influence of a few glasses of wine. Fine, a bottle.

The pile of unopened boxes stood proudly next to the front door, and she cringed every single time she walked by. She needed adult supervision. And more money to fund her late-night one-click frenzies.

The doorbell chimed again. It was one thing she hated about her house—you couldn't peek around the doorframe of any of the rooms without being busted by whomever stood waiting on the porch. She'd always talked about putting frosted glass in the door, or blinds, or a security camera, or trying to do *something* to give herself a little more time to decide on whether she actually wanted to open the door or not.

But, like so many other honey-do projects around the

house, she was the only "honey" around, and by the time she got done with her day, or week, she just couldn't "do."

Elliott's piercing stare caught her through the panes of glass surrounding the door. He clutched a bag from her favorite Greek restaurant which he held up for her to see. He raised his eyebrows and cocked his head.

His face said *What's it gonna be, Clare Bear?* and her grumbling stomach said *Hell-to-the-motherfuckin-yeah,* so she opened the door with a sigh.

She hated how well he knew her.

"Let me guess..." She popped her hip as she let him into the house. "You just so happened to be passing by somewhere you had no idea I'd be, with food from our favorite Greek place?"

"Close." He stepped out of her way so she could close the door behind him. "I stopped and saw your mom to ask her where you lived."

Well, shit. He was either brave, or stupid. Having known him as a child she could confirm it was, in fact, a mixture of both. But going to see Mom. Wow. That was...something.

"And she let you out alive?"

He chuckled as she led the way into the kitchen. "Barely. I figured it was time for me to square away some outstanding issues she and I had."

Reaching into the cabinet, she rose on her tiptoes and grabbed two plates with a clink. "Oh, yeah?" She couldn't turn to look at his face, or he'd see how red her cheeks were. He could probably hear her heart thudding already.

The only thing he could have to talk to Mom about was her.

"Yeah. Seems she and I had some things to lay out and go over."

Interesting.

And yet she hadn't called to warn Clare that he'd run

the parental gauntlet and was on his way over. Traitor. She could have at least given her a heads up so he didn't find Clare when her home looked like a tornado had passed through it.

And she'd have liked a shower, or the choice to wear something other than hot pink yoga pants and her *Feminism is my second favorite F-word* shirt. Oh God. When was the last time she even washed her hair? Could she sniff her underarm without him seeing? Probably not.

"And how did that go?" Stay cool. Breathe. She'd figure out her matricide plans later—or, if she opted for a less homicidal path, then at least come up with a way for Mom and Dad to make it up to her.

"I'm here, aren't I?"

"Fair point." He had obviously won Mom over with whatever he had said to her. And he'd also obviously been apologetic enough for her parents not to chop his body into tiny pieces and hide him in the woods for breaking their daughter's heart.

She pointed a plate at him and narrowed her glare. "You could have called. Given me a few minutes to pick up the house." She smoothed out her hair. "At least shower. There was no guarantee I'd even let you in."

He nodded solemnly. "We talked about it, but ultimately your mom said if I warned you, you'd have come up with eleventy million excuses, hidden, or fled." He shrugged. "She's not wrong. And I'm more scared of her than you. Hell, I'm more scared of her than your dad. She also said when your ex takes Mason, and Cat goes to her friends, you clean up right away so you can enjoy the weekend without having a mess hanging over your head."

He pulled packages from the bag as she placed the plates on the table.

"She did, huh? What else did she say?"

He tapped the side of his nose as he plopped a package onto her plate. "That's between her and me."

"Wine?"

He arched a brow. "Sure."

She picked up the bottle of red she'd opened and left on the counter to breathe, grabbed two glasses, and sank onto her chair with all the grace of an elephant. "You're really not going to tell me what you talked about with Mom and Dad?"

He shrugged, unwrapping his shawarma and taking a huge bite. When he'd finished chewing and moaning like it was the best thing he'd ever had in his mouth, he took a sip of wine. "I told them I'd seen you and wanted to see you again."

Great. Mom would be cranky that she hadn't mentioned running into him at the pharmacy. She'd think Clare was keeping their store encounter a secret for some reason and would make it into something it wasn't. Ugh.

Heat skittered up her spine. It absolutely wasn't anything. Nope. Nothing. At all. She tore a piece of still-warm pita in two and dragged it through the container of hummus before pointing it at him. "You have my number. You could have called."

"You'd have said no."

"You don't know that."

He totally did know that. She absolutely, positively, definitely would have said no.

"I do too know that. I know you. I figured I needed reinforcements."

"And Greek food." She gestured at her gyro and couldn't help but laugh as she shook her head. "I can't believe you went to see Mom and Dad."

"Neither could they. You might be surprised to learn that having a heartbroken daughter is something that's engrained in their memories. I'm amazed your dad didn't club me to death with his baseball bat. I wasn't expecting to make it out alive."

She laughed again at the image. Daddy could have done it, and they both knew it, too.

"I told her I wanted to take you out, and she shook her head. Surprisingly not because it was *me* wanting to take you out, but she said you don't go out much. She said that between work and the kids, any free time you have... Well, you...uh...just want to spend it..."

"Say it." She tipped her glass at him, giving him permission to repeat what Clare had heard Mom say almost weekly since she had gotten divorced.

"She said you were a hermit." He winced. "That if I wanted to see you I'd need to go to you, and bring food. The last part I already knew, though. She told me to make sure I at least pretended to bring vegetables. Hence the gyro and hummus."

"I'm so predictable." She'd always been easy to win over with the promise of a good meal. "So what are you really doing here, Elliott?" As fun as the back and forth about her parents was, this wasn't the reason he'd come.

He pointed at his shawarma as she popped another bite of pita into her mouth. Damn. It really was delicious. "Food first."

There was nowhere better he could have brought food from. Starting strong out of the gate. Obviously he wanted to butter her up for something, and she was only too open to being buttered—especially if it was with a delicious gyro.

She hadn't had one in so long she'd almost forgotten how much she loved it. Between delicious, orgasm-noise-making bites, they chatted about Mason's hockey, Cat's college options, a bit about his divorce and how they'd both been cheated on.

They'd both become walking stereotypes.

Cramming the trash back into the paper bag he'd brought dinner in, his face turned serious. "I saw some supplies out in the yard. And your mom said you have some stuff to do around the house, stuff that you—and I'm quoting now—can't or won't do by yourself." He shrugged. "Don't shoot the messenger."

Her stomach hardened. "I'm perfectly capable of taking care of myself, Eli."

He held his hands up. "I never said you couldn't, Ceecee. But if you wanted a little help." He lifted his arms and flexed his biceps. "I have a full hockey team of strong, young men who could probably help."

She burst out laughing. "So you're volunteering your kids, not yourself."

"The offer's there if you want it. I'm pretty good with a hammer." His brow twitched at the innuendo.

I bet you are. "Is that why you came over? Greek food and DIY?"

Reaching into his back pocket, he shook his head. "Actually, I wanted to bring you this." He smoothed out a worn and yellowing piece of paper and her heart stopped. Surely not.

"No." The word fell from her lips on a gasp. "You've kept that all this time?"

He nodded, his expression unreadable.

Realization crawled over her skin like ants. "You can't hold me to anything from back then, Elliott. That's not fair."

Another nod. "That's true, I can't. But I'm still gonna." He turned the page to face her and the words *Clare and Elliott's BHAG List* were written across the top in purple marker.

"Big hairy audacious goals." Her voice was barely a whisper as she reached out but didn't touch the paper in case it might somehow bite her.

"When was the last time you did something new or exciting, or something for yourself?"

When she opened her mouth to speak, he quirked a brow. "And sitting at the bar with a book and a basket of fried cheese doesn't count."

"It does, too!" Her mouth moved against his palm as she spoke, but he still didn't move, so she licked it.

"Ew. Still as gross as ever." He wiped his hand on his thigh.

"Still as annoying as ever."

"We made this list when the world was our oyster, Clare. When we had enormous dreams and even more confidence that we could actually reach them. I'm game to knock a few things off it if you are." His hazel eyes sparkled as he spoke and the more he spoke, the faster his words came, like they were fueled by the excitement of the teenager who had helped craft the list all those years ago. "Unless you're chicken."

Ugh. She hated when he baited her. He knew her too well. She sipped on her wine as she scanned the list. "We're too old for some of these things, Eli. Too old and too broke."

"And you're going to make up any excuse you can not to step out of your comfort zone. We can use some creative license on some of the crazier ideas. We've both already done number fifteen." He grunted, bitterness coating his words. "You can cross that one off."

#15—Get married.

He was right, they had. At the time they'd written it, she'd always assumed they'd marry each other, not other people. He produced a purple marker from his pocket and handed it to her. "You in?"

She stared at the list again. "I think—"

He smacked the table. "Stop thinking. We weren't thinking when we wrote this list, we were *feeling*. What are you feeling?"

She covered her face with her hands. "Scared? Embarrassed? Ashamed?" Heavy tears slid down her cheeks. She hated where she was in life, and more than that, she hated that he was still Elliott, the person who managed to make her dig deep, to feel deep, and who never let her hide, not even from herself.

"I hate you." But not really.

He didn't say anything, just waited in silence for her tears to stop. She wiped her face, took the marker he was still holding, and crossed off number fifteen. Putting the cap back on the pen she tapped it on the list. "We did number twenty-nine, too."

#29—Write a letter to yourself to open in ten years.

"I don't know where we put them. I'd guess they're in Mom and Dad's attic somewhere if they survived the ages, but we did it." She ticked off twenty nine, and a weird look flickered across Elliott's face. "What?"

With a deep breath he dug back into his pocket. Oh God. No. He didn't. He couldn't. Fuck. He totally did.

The sight of the faded pink envelope made her heart quicken. "How?"

"You want the truth? Or you want me to tell you it was in your mom's attic?"

A fresh wave of tears trickled down her cheeks as she took the envelope from him.

"I kept them in a box under my bed." His quiet admission and the weight of everything else unsaid pressed on her chest. He'd kept them. The list, the letters, their history, her mauled fucking heart, he'd kept it all.

What the fuck did that mean?

She slid the envelope to the side of the table while she dipped her finger into the hummus and sucked it off her fingertip. She wasn't hungry anymore, it was just something to do, something to distract her from the envelope, from the feelings welling in her chest and the tears still close to the surface.

She'd open it later, when she was alone, when he couldn't read her like a fucking book.

"We can check off number eighteen too." She put a line through the box next to it.

He chuckled. "I didn't win the Stanley Cup."

"That's true. But you won the Frozen Four—as a player and a coach—and you won the Hobey Baker memorial award."

His eyebrows shot up and his eyes widened.

She nodded smugly. "I pay attention. I know that the Hobey is the most prestigious award in college hockey. It recognizes the top NCAA DI men's ice hockey player in the country." She'd memorized the spiel when he'd won it.

"But wait—hockey skills and stats aren't the only criteria, no sir. The Hobey is awarded to the player that most embodies a variety of qualities, including sportsmanship and character." She grinned at him.

The flush that spread up his neck and into his cheeks was adorable. He'd never been good at taking compliments. "I can't believe you kept up with my career."

She shrugged. She'd absorbed every single news story she could find about him while he was away. She watched away games, read blogs and hockey forums, she'd even ordered a jersey with his name on it when he'd gotten to the AHL.

"You also got the Dudley Garrett Memorial Award for rookie of the year when you moved up into the AHL."

He winced. "A short-lived career in the minor leagues."

"Don't downplay your accomplishments. Each one is important. Plus, they're all there in black and white on HockeyDB.com." She wagged a finger. "You played hard, you won a ton of things. Sure, it's not quite the Stanley Cup, but it's worthy of a check mark on our list. You basically won everything that was in your path along the way. And I bet if you'd gone to the NHL you'd have won the Colin Smythe *and* Lord Stanley."

"Conn."

Her brows dipped into a frown. "Huh? Colin Smythe Conn?"

"Conn Smythe is the trophy, Colin's better known brother...or something." He winked at her. "But I appreciate the ego stroking." He sighed. "Okay, we can cross it out, but note my reluctance."

"Why? You ignored my reluctance when you put this damn list in front of me."

"True story."

"There is no Colin Smythe, is there?"

"I mean... there might be... but there's no hockey trophy for him. It's okay, even hockey players get confused about who the trophies are for. I'm sure if there *is* a Colin Smythe he's a lovely man and deserves to have a cup named in his honor."

She giggled as another envelope came out of his back pocket.

"Seriously? How much shit do you have in your pockets? Be glad you're not wearing women's jeans, our pockets suck."

He tapped the envelope against his palm, not meeting her eyes. "I, uh..." He swept his hand down the back of his neck and cleared his throat.

"What is it?"

"Tickets. For the Snow Pirates. I figured Mason might want to go to the game next weekend. I understand if you're busy and you can't. I didn't mean to presume, but I wanted to...just in case, y'know?"

His babbling was as delightful as his blushing. "Thank you. Mason will shit his pants. He loves going to watch you guys. Granted, he usually goes with his dad, but I could be the cool mom for a change."

She leaned to her left pointing the envelope of tickets at

his pants. "What else you got back there? Is this where you pull a lamp from your ass pocket a la Mary Poppins?"

"Uh. I..."

"Elliott, I swear to all that's holy if you have a lamp in the ass pocket of your jeans I'm writing to every women's clothing company I can think of to demand they right the injustice. We can't even cram Chapstick in ours."

He laughed and his shoulders relaxed. "No, it's just... It's not a lamp, but I do have something else." He reached into the paper bag the food came in and pulled out a small book—*Easy Origami*—and a pack of colored paper. "I ordered these for myself, too. I figured we could work on number sixteen."

#16—Make an origami animal.

She rolled her eyes. "How'd you know I was going to say yes?"

"I didn't. And you still haven't said yes. I just figured you were never one to back down from a challenge and if I went ahead and did the list without you I'd be the winner and you'd hate it."

"I..."

He pointed at her. "Don't even lie about it, Ceecee. We both know you can be competitive as fuck."

She laughed and held her hands up. "I used to be, now I leave that to my kids. But I'd definitely hate it if you did our list alone."

He held out the origami book and colored paper. "Is that a yes?"

"It's a yes."

CHAPTER 6
Elliott

It turned out that number sixteen was fucking hard, as proven by the papercuts dotted across Elliott's fingers. All he wanted to do was make a delicate little paper swan, but that sucker just kept evading him. His chunky fingers and the tiny paper—he just kept fucking it up.

How hard was it to fold fucking paper?

Apparently very.

He wasn't giving up, though, nor was he going to back down and try something easier to make. The goddamn swan was going to happen. He'd wanted to make one since he was fourteen years old, and a few of the most painful cuts of his life weren't going to deter him.

He'd broken bones, torn ligaments, had head wounds that bled profusely, but there was something about the tiniest of papercuts that hurt more than all of them combined. He sucked his throbbing index finger with a groan.

Perhaps it had less to do with the size of his hands, or his skills at folding small colored paper into beautiful pieces of art, and more to do with the fact that Clare Reynolds was back in his head, in his life, in his goddamn space, and he couldn't concentrate on diddly squat. If he was truly honest with himself, she'd never really been out of it, at least mentally, but her physical presence was turning him upside down and inside out.

While he'd loved Denise a lot, enough to marry her, he'd unknowingly given a piece of himself to Clare when they were just kids, and even if he wanted to, he could never get it back.

Clare sat somewhere in the stands behind him with her son, watching the game.

His game. His team. In his barn.

He swallowed. His stomach was in knots—and not for any reason linked with hockey. The team looked good: better, stronger. He'd go so far as to say they were starting to adjust to the loss of Morgan, Morrison and O'Brien, but he didn't want to tempt fate by saying it out loud.

Thankfully, they were playing Cedar Rapids and not Alabama. The bad blood between his boys and Johnny White for abandoning them when he transferred after winning the Frozen Four, bumped up Elliott's blood pressure beyond acceptable limits.

The Raccoons on the other hand, they could handle just fine. Mostly. They had a couple of interesting rookies he'd be keeping his eye on throughout the season, but for the most part, they were an enemy his guys knew how to handle.

Heat crawled up the back of his neck. Was she watching him? Was she impressed by his team? Was Mason? He'd arranged for a couple of the players to sign some autographs for Mason when the game was over, but he was questioning himself. Was it too much of a flex?

He didn't want to be an asshole, but at the same time, the kid was clearly a fan of the sport and enthusiastic about playing. But maybe he had no interest in the Snow Pirates, and realistically speaking, if he wanted signatures, or even to meet the players, Coach Morrison had an in with his friends still on the team.

It was too much, wasn't it?

Shit. Shit. Shitting fucking fuck.

He'd missed a goal while he'd been questioning his life choices. Thankfully it was his own team so he didn't need to bust anyone's balls for fucking up, but until the commentator announced who scored, he was clueless.

It was time to bust his own balls, to get his head out of his ass, and back in the game. Figuring out where the boundaries with Clare and her kid were, figuring out how to protect himself from the woman who had already betrayed him once before, it would all have to wait.

It was another unassisted goal for the rookie, Theo. Elliott rolled his eyes. The kid plopped down onto the bench with a shit eating grin on his face like he'd single handedly won the Stanley Cup.

But there was no "I" in team. Being a whiz on the ice, scoring a bunch of fancy goals was all well and good, but if you couldn't work well as part of a team to ensure the "W" at the end of sixty minutes of play then it meant nothing.

Theo needed a lesson in humility, teamwork. Elliott had seen kids like him before, and he'd see them again. It was his job to knock the overconfident asshole out of him and encourage the skillful player, while not breaking his spirit. It was a fine line to walk.

As the second period drew close to an end, Lincoln Scott, team captain and son of a former NHL superstar, elbowed Russell and jerked his chin at Theo. Sometimes players took it upon themselves to teach the assholes a lesson. To show them what it was like when they played for the name on the back of their shirt instead of the logo on the front.

Perhaps Theo needed a reminder that without his team

watching his six, his ability to score goals would be greatly hindered.

They were up 2-0 with a period still to play, realistically, it was their game to lose. And a bone-deep feeling from decades of hockey experience told him they were losing this one.

As much as he hated losing a game, sometimes you handed over the battle in order to win the war. If Theo got his head out of his ass and learned to play nice with the other children in the sandbox, their team could be unstoppable.

Off the bench and back on the ice, Theo claimed possession of the puck yet again. Dominated the space. He skated up the wing—not another Snow Pirate to be seen anywhere near him. Christ, the kid was fast. As he approached the blue line, a Raccoon appeared by his side and threw him into the boards with a monumental hip check.

Theo crumpled like a slinky down stairs and the spectators hissed in sympathy. On his way back to the bench, number two for the Cedar Rapids Raccoons, defenseman Artemis de la Peña, subtly fist-bumped Lincoln Scott. To most people watching, the defenseman nearly crashed into the Captain of the Snow Pirates, but Elliott wasn't most people.

Had Lincoln somehow encouraged Artemis to throw a heavy check at Theo in a bid to teach him a lesson? Any other player on the team and he'd have believed it without hesitation, but Linc? Wow. Things must have been worse in the locker room than he thought. Elliott shook his head as Theo skated like Bambi on ice back to the bench. It could have been worse. Linc could have asked *two* of the de la Peña brothers to check Theo—at the same fucking time.

While Apollo de la Peña was a forward, he and his twin brother, Artemis made quite the checking duo when they wanted to. Most people knew to stay well clear. Apparently Theo hadn't done his homework. And clearly Lincoln was more aware of Theo's shortcomings than Elliott had realized.

As Linc climbed onto the bench, Elliott leaned close so only he could hear. "Wanna tell me what the hell kind of shit you're pulling out there, *Captain?*"

Linc kept his eyes on the game as he gave a one-shoulder shrug. "Team building."

Elliott snorted and Theo erupted. "Is no one gonna go after that asshole for the hit on me?"

Silence. You could cut the tension with a knife. Or a hockey skate.

"Seriously?" The rookie's voice rose with his indignation. Elliott could hear the subtext. The audacity. Why would his team not jump to the defense of their star player? Gasp. Hand-on-forehead. Dramatic wail.

The kid was seconds from either throwing down a "don't you know who I am?" or a "you'd all be fucked without me" comment. His shoulders were square and his jaw, firm. When he stood up, Linc reached over and tugged the hem of his jersey, hard, forcing the rookie to splat back onto the bench. Linc switched places with Russell and leaned close to Theo's ear, but Elliott couldn't hear what was said.

The rookie stayed quiet, but anger radiated from Theo as he took his next shift.

"What'd you say to him?" Elliott couldn't help but be curious.

Linc shrugged. "Just that on this team we don't play for the names on the back of the shirt. No matter how good we might be by ourselves. I just reminded him that even the greatest hockey players in the world can't do shit without the help and support of their team."

Elliott nodded. Linc was right. His method of delivering the lesson to Theo was risky—he could have gotten seriously hurt if de la Peña hadn't landed the hit right—but what he'd said was true.

"I told him we'd be only too happy to have his back,

against the de la Peña brothers or anyone else who fucked with him, as long as he had ours. And right now, he doesn't."

Pride swelled in Elliott's chest at the growth he'd seen in Linc since he joined the team. So many of the kids had stepped up over the years, but few had stepped up in a way that left their mark on the team like Linc had, like Will had.

True leadership was hard to find, but the team was rallying around Linc like he'd been born to lead. Just like his father.

He smacked a hand on Linc's shoulder. "I'm proud of you for taking your responsibilities seriously, Linc. But that hit could have gone wrong and ended up with Theo getting hurt. How did you know de la Peña would help?"

Linc laughed. "After what happened during pre-season?"

His stomach dropped. "What happened during pre-season?"

"I need to get back on the ice, Coach."

He didn't like it when his players kept shit from him, but Elliott couldn't say he hadn't gotten up to no good when he played college hockey, so he let it slide. "He could have done real damage out there, Lincoln."

"De la Peña knew to be careful." Linc spoke quietly and turned his head, probably to make sure no one was listening.

"And how many times have you done something carefully on the ice that produced an unexpected result?"

Linc winced. Message received. "Sorry, Coach."

"Let's just hope Theo got the memo, okay?"

Linc nodded, took his next shift, and led the team to a 3-1 victory over Cedar Rapids. A knot of anxiety that had been weighing heavily in Elliott's abdomen unraveled at the final buzzer. He hadn't realized how much he'd wanted to impress Clare until the team had taken to the ice.

What a fucking idiot. Clearly, the matter of personal pride as an athlete was hard to shake, even as a coach. But it all went through the roof when it came to impressing his girl.

His girl. It had been an age since he called her that, even to himself.

They'd won, they'd given the crowd a fun game to watch, and he could face Clare without her looking at him with pity swimming in her eyes. Was there anything worse?

"Great game, Coach." She bumped her hip against his when he came to a stop next to her in the corridor outside the locker room.

"Thanks. Where's Mason?"

She jerked her thumb over her shoulder toward the locker room door. "One of the players asked if he wanted to take a look around behind the scenes while the rest of the team got dressed. Then he'd take him for autographs and to get a jersey left aside for him." She folded her arms and arched a brow. "You know anything about that?"

His mouth dried up. "It's too much, right?" He nodded before she had a chance to answer. "Totally too much. I just... I dunno, I guess I wanted to make it special for him."

He'd be lying if he said he didn't want to stick it to Mason's dad, Clare's ex, just a little. Okay, a lot. Any guy who left her for another woman, was an idiot who deserved everything he got.

Was he showing off a little in hopes that Mason would talk about how it was the best night of his entire life? Sure. Did he give a flying fuck? Nope.

Was he also hoping to melt the inch-thick ice around Clare's heart and nudge her toward forgiving him? Absolutely. The more he saw of her, the more he realized just how much he missed his best friend and partner in crime.

Her frown flickered, a small smile teasing at the corner of her lips. "You've always been a bit flashy." She shook her head.

"I have not!" He clutched his chest like she'd struck him. Okay, he totally was prone to being somewhat OTT. But no one liked to be reminded of their flaws—even if it was by beautiful women from their childhood.

"Uh huh. Do you want me to call Suzy what's-her-name? I'm sure she'll confirm that for those twenty-nine days she was your girlfriend you showered her with every stereotypical gift under the sun."

He swallowed the barbs at the back of his throat, his skin prickling at her subtle reminder that you couldn't buy love, or —as it turned out with Denise—loyalty, either. Holding up a hand, he forced a chuckle.

"It's good. You want something warm to drink while we wait?"

She nodded and he took the opportunity to escape to the coffee machine to grab her a drink. He needed to catch his breath. The reminder that he'd essentially been duped by his ex, and then taken to the cleaners for everything he was worth, lay heavily in his stomach.

An hour later, Theo emerged from the locker room with a wide-eyed and red-cheeked Mason. "Mom, Mom! Theo said he'll come skating with me sometime." The excitement in the kid's voice was tangible and Elliott almost swallowed his tongue at the thought that Theo was offering to do something for someone else.

Theo rubbed the back of his neck, his cheeks going as red as Mason's, and shrugged. "I have a little brother. He loves hockey too. I'd like to think someone will take care of him when he's old enough to play." He shrugged again and offered his fist to Mason. "Can't wait to hang out, bud. I'll give Coach my cell number so we can figure something out, okay?"

Wonders would never cease. Maybe there was hope for the rookie yet. Mason nodded, his jaw hanging wide open like God himself had suggested they hang out together. Theo ruffled Mason's hair before heading back into the locker room.

"Mom. Look." Mason's voice still held a wonder that

warmed Elliott's chest. Lincoln Scott had brought in an old game worn shirt and signed it for the kid, and Elliott had found a poster that he'd given to Mason for the rest of the team to sign.

"Lincoln Scott gave this to me. He played with Coach Morrison, Mom. He's the team captain." He spoke to her like she knew nothing about the team at all. Did he know she used to go to every one of Elliott's games when they were younger—and most of his practices, too?

She probably knew the rules even better than he did. Had she given up on the game when he'd gone away? The familiar pang of guilt struck deep in his chest. If only he had the chance for a do-over. He'd still have left, still have chased his dream, but he'd have done more, tried harder to keep his friendship with Clare while he did.

Mason chattered away about each of the players, what they did on the team, and things they said to him as they were signing his poster. If Elliott could change the past, Mason and Catriona wouldn't exist, either. He didn't know much about kids, but if they were anything like their mom, they were both pretty great.

Mom took great pleasure in reminding him that everything happened for a reason. Perhaps Clare would forgive him. Perhaps this was his chance for a do-over. Perhaps, this time, he wouldn't fuck it up.

"Who wants milkshakes?"

Mason fist pumped and hissed out, "Yessssss. Can we, Mom? Please?"

Clare pinned Elliott with a glare that said, "thanks, asshole, now I can't say no." And Elliott made a mental note not to speak out of turn again in the future. Clearing everything through mom-Clare was going to be at the top of his to-do list going forward.

Through a tight-lipped smile she shook her head. "Sorry,

Mase-Mallow. But it's getting late and it's a school night. Maybe next time, okay?"

Mason's body tensed. "But Mom…"

Clare's whole body sagged under the weight of Mason's sigh. "You've had a fantastic evening, Mason. Please be grateful for that, and don't make this a thing."

"Dad would let me."

What a master manipulator. Points to the kid for trying, but Elliott clenched his jaw so he didn't interfere. Clare didn't need him making things worse. Again.

"You're not here with your father, Mason, you're here with me. And I say no. Please respect that."

"I hate you." Mason's growl drained the color from Clare's face, her blue eyes darkened, and her throat bobbed as she swallowed.

"Mason. I think you owe your mom an apology for your behavior." He couldn't take it anymore. He couldn't watch this teenage terror hurt Clare and stay silent. She'd deflated so much it hurt to look at her.

Mason grunted and took off toward the exit.

"Sorry." He leaned close to her and spoke softly so Mason couldn't hear what he said. "I shouldn't have thought out loud. I'll check with you in the future."

Her shoulders lowered from her ears and her jaw loosened. "Thanks. I'd appreciate that. I have enough undermining on my hands with Mason's dad. And thanks for sticking up for me."

Of course he'd stuck up for her. As nice as the kid was, he was being a spoiled little shit. Clare didn't deserve to be treated like that just because she was being a responsible parent.

"You're not mad?"

She shook her head and tears escaped her welling eyes, leaving tracks down her cheeks. "Truthfully it's kind of a relief."

The picture he was getting suggested no one had ever fought for her, and that made him sick to his stomach. He fought every urge to reach out and pull her to him. He didn't care what they did together, he just wanted to be with her, seeing her smile, interact with her kids, being with her made him feel better.

All he needed to do was figure out how to return the favor and earn her forgiveness for breaking her heart all those years ago.

CHAPTER 7
Elliott

> Elliott: I'm really sorry, Clare. I can't help you right now.

She hadn't asked him for much, just for him to pick up Mason from school, take him home to grab his gear, then over to the rink for hockey practice. But as much as he wished he could, Elliott couldn't drop things at a moment's notice and step up to help her. Pressing "send" was hard. His gut twisted. But it was what it was. He just couldn't help her.

Sitting in IHOP waiting for a late-as-usual Denise to show up for some life-or-death, urgent meeting that she *absolutely* needed to happen. He was pissed. He'd rescheduled visiting Mom at the nursing home for the second time in a week, and while he felt bad for saying no to Clare, he had his own shit going on.

Clare had confided in him that she'd lost most of her friends in the divorce, her parents were retiring to Florida before the end of the year so they wouldn't be able to help out with the kids or her busy, single, hockey mom life for much longer, and her ex was an unreliable asshole who seemed intent on deliberately making her life harder. According to her, his family wasn't much better, either.

Having spoken at length with her parents, he knew that meant her life was scheduled down to the hour, some days even the minute, and it didn't allow for getting stuck at work, getting a flat tire, or even taking a long bath. There was no room for spontaneity, or the unexpected. She took care of her business and kept all the plates spinning. He had no idea how she did it all.

> Clare: It's fine. I'll figure it out.

Ouch. Shots fired, yet again. Clare Reynold's passive aggression was a thing of legend. The subtext was that he was just another person to let her down when she needed someone. That he'd let her down again. He didn't remember her being quite so unreasonable, however.

Sure, she was stuck at work, dealing with some kind of medical billing emergency and needed help. But maybe if she'd given enough of a crap to ask, he'd have told her that he was trying to balance a money-grabbing ex, a sick mother, and a team that were hopefully past the cutting teeth phase of their season.

His life wasn't exactly a cakewalk either.

Taking a sip of his coffee, he stared at Clare's reply. "Lio." Denise took her seat across the booth from him as he cringed. He hated the nickname, and she knew it. That probably should have been his first clue that the relationship was doomed from the get-go—she was never one to make any kind of allowance or respect his boundaries.

"Thanks for coming. Tim is going to Outdoor World and circling back to pick me up, so I'll make this quick."

Fucking her boss didn't exactly help matters either.

Grinding his teeth to stop a caustic reply from escaping his lips, he grunted.

"I need to refinance the house. And I can't do that with your name on it. I need for you to sign these papers so I can move forward okay?"

He accepted the manila envelope across the table and tapped it against his palm. "And you couldn't have just dropped this off at the house, or the rink? You had to drag me across town to hand me an envelope?"

She shrugged and her cheeks turned pink. Why did everything have to be overly complicated with the woman? Was it all a power play for her?

Her phone lit up on the table. "That's Tim. He's outside."

"So when you said it was life-or-death and you needed to talk to me over coffee, what you *actually* meant was you needed to hand me an envelope?"

"I—"

He held up a hand. "Just go, Dee. I don't want to hear it."

She huffed, her facing turning a darker shade of red, and folded her arms. "Don't be like that, Lio."

"Stop calling me that," he ground out through still-gritted teeth, his temples pulsing.

Leaning forward, she gripped his forearm. "Sorry. Hard to break the habit of a lifetime, right?" A nasal giggle fell heavily between them. "I wanted to see you."

"Why?" If he stared any harder at the coffee cup next to his arm, he'd pierce a hole in it. Her hand was still on his arm and she squeezed.

"Can't a girl just want to see her ex?" She pulled her arm back, flicking her hand like it was a totally normal request. Her phone lit up again. "I really need to go." She nibbled on her bottom lip. "I don't like to keep him waiting."

But she didn't mind hauling Elliott across town for no fucking reason. He *could* be visiting with Mom, he *could* be helping Clare out with Mason, hell, he could be sitting balls-out on the sofa watching porn for fuck's sake. But instead, he was sitting drinking luke-warm coffee and being driven insane by the smell of pancakes he thought he'd be having for dinner with his ex.

He shuddered. She stood.

"I'm pissed, Dee. This isn't okay, and it won't happen again, you hear me?"

Her eyes widened.

"But you always come when I call."

He nodded, flaring his nostrils. "Past tense. It stops now. No more. You've cried wolf one too many times and I'm done. I have a life, I have shit to do, responsibilities. I don't owe you anything. You took the best years of my life and left me broke. We aren't friends."

Each word made her flinch as her jaw hung open.

"I'm supposed to be visiting Mom. The nurse said today was a good day, she doesn't have those very often anymore, and I'm here with *you*. We're done, Dee." He nodded again. "I'm done."

She rolled her lips, her eyes flaring. "Fine. Sign the fucking papers and we never have to see each other again."

He had so many questions. Was she planning on selling at last? They'd agreed to sell up and split the money fifty-fifty. It would be enough to clear his debts and bail him out of hot water. But every time he brought up the subject, she gave him excuse after excuse.

He wouldn't want to see her homeless, *right*?

Despite her meeting him at the office, her precious Tim now had no job, no home, and no prospects. He was living in their marital home, with Elliott's ex-wife, while Elliott lived in a shitty one-bedroom apartment with damp in the walls because his parent's house was too far away from his job. Fucking Tim.

"I'll read them, sign them, and drop them off when I'm done."

"Don't take too long." She slid a thumbnail between her teeth. "We need to get it sorted out, ASAP, mmkay?" Blowing him a kiss, she turned and sashayed out of the diner.

Was she fucking kidding?

"Would you like a refill?" A server stopped at his table.

"Got anything stronger?" Her snicker made his head snap up. "Sorry. I didn't mean that."

"Yes, you did." The white-haired, elderly woman grinned at him. "Lemme fix you a stack. It's not a shot of whiskey, but it might make you feel a bit better."

Damn straight, it would. Pancakes for one sounded pretty damn delicious.

He gave her a warm smile. "Thanks, Maisy. I'd appreciate it."

With a nod, she topped up his mug with fresh coffee and left him alone to his envelope. Sliding the pages out onto the table he wondered how his life had been reduced to a few pieces of paper and fluffy pancakes alone in a well-loved diner.

Raking his hand through his hair, he scanned the first page. It looked simple enough, but he'd still want his lawyer to look it all over and make sure Denise wasn't co-opting him into a kidney removal or something more sinister.

Page two and three were more of the same, with a small pink Post It flagging on page three where she wanted him to sign. Now that his blood pressure was starting to return to normal, he wondered why she needed to refinance, and why his name needed to be taken off the damn house to do so. It wasn't adding up. He smelled a rat. A Tim-sized rat.

Page three was stuck to page four, and when he tugged to separate them, another pink Post It highlighted a space for another signature.

Only this time it wasn't his. Every drop of blood rushed to

the surface of his body as he vibrated with rage. The name staring back at him was Denise's current beau, Tim Delaney.

Swallowing down the burning bile at the back of his throat, he gripped the page like it might flutter away or disappear. Was she really taking *his* name off the mortgage so she could put that freeloading piece of shit's name on instead?

Did she think he was born yesterday? That he wouldn't question it? That she could somehow pull a switcheroo and he just wouldn't notice that he no longer co-owned a house?

Fuck.

Over his dead and decaying fucking body would that asshole get Elliott's house.

His hands trembled, making the page jitter and twitch. But he definitely wasn't seeing things. The more he scanned and rescanned the words the more furious he became. What the fuck did she think she was doing? She'd almost had him fooled, too. There was a time he'd have blindly signed the paper and handed it to her without reading the fine print.

That's probably what she'd banked on.

Conniving bitch.

Fuck. There'd been a time when he'd have done anything for her. Literally anything. Kidney removal and all. Both of them.

Hell, if she'd asked him to, he'd have carved them out with no anesthetic and a fucking spoon. Not anymore.

His phone rang on the table. Clare. With a sigh, he flexed his jaw and hit the green button.

"Eli, I'm sorry to keep bugging you but..." Her tense voice cracked as she trailed off. "I'm desperate. I have someone picking Mason up from school, but I was wondering if you could bring him home after practice. I wouldn't ask but—"

"I said I can't help you, Clare." His words burst out on a growl.

"Of course. I... I... I'm sorry for asking—"

He pushed the red button and slammed both the paper, and the phone onto the table, causing his mug to clink and the coffee to slosh over the side. He snapped a picture of the paperwork and emailed it to his lawyer with a note that he'd drop the originals off tomorrow during business hours. The man never slept and worked 24-7 so he'd probably have them read by the time Elliott handed him the pages.

Maybe he was misreading it, maybe she wasn't trying to fuck him with his pants on, maybe it just looked like it and there was a perfectly reasonable explanation as to why she wanted his name off the house.

And maybe pigs could fly.

Denise had unknowingly declared war, and he was done with her bullshit. It was time to get her the fuck out of that house and figure out his finances once and for all. He just needed to figure out how.

"I'm so sorry."

Clare's narrowed eyes, folded arms, and pursed lips suggested she wasn't buying his lame-ass apology. "You hung up on me."

He nodded. He had done that. "I did. I'm sorry for that, too."

The kids were finishing up on the ice, but practice wasn't quite over yet. Elliott had come to the rink specifically to apologize to her for being an asshat. That had to count for something, right?

The flickering fury in her eyes told him no, it didn't count for anything.

"Clare, I..." He rubbed the back of his neck with his palm. "I'm going through some shit right now. I know that's not an excuse, but my mom..."

Her face softened. So she knew.

She nodded. "Mom said she'd been recently moved into an assisted living facility."

He could read her like a book. She knew more than that. She knew that Mom was deteriorating, she knew Dad was struggling at home alone but too stubborn to move in somewhere with Elliott, or sell their home and move somewhere more manageable.

She probably also knew that if one died, the other would die of a broken heart. His stomach clenched. "It's more than that. And Denise is being…well, Denise."

The words stuck in his throat. He didn't want to talk to Clare about Denise. He didn't want her thinking that Denise still held space in his life. She didn't. It was over between them.

"She's trying to take the house." He shrugged. "She had nowhere to go, y'know? I thought letting her live there until she figured something else out, until she was in a better position to sell, was the noble thing to do."

He frowned. "Sorry, this isn't… I shouldn't…" He blew out a puff of air and took a step toward her. "My point is that none of this is your fault. I was entirely out of line snapping at you and hanging up on you and…"

Was it getting hotter in the rink? Or was the brewing storm still in her eyes producing enough heat to crank up his body temp?

Will blew his whistle and the kids reset for another drill on the ice.

Clare covered Elliott's mouth with her delicate fingers and gave him a soft smile. "I won't say it's okay, because it isn't. I definitely didn't deserve your ire earlier. And I admit, I wanted to scream obscenities at you when you put the phone down on me. In fact, I might have yelled cusswords, but I'll neither confirm nor deny it."

She shrugged, the edges of her smile tugging higher. "But I

accept your apology. I can't imagine the stress you're under right now. But I figured out my emergency by myself. I'm sorry for calling you. I couldn't think of anyone else to help out."

His stomach dropped. Her pale face had fallen from fury to sympathy, to something close to fear, maybe even shame, in a matter of seconds. He took another step forward and cupped her cheek. Her skin was so fucking soft against his palm. Was the rest of her skin as soft? His dick twitched at the thought of nestling between her ass cheeks.

"I don't want you to apologize. I want to be there for you where I can." He leaned closer to her, he needed her to know, to know everything. Brushing his nose against the side of hers, his muscles relaxed, her body did too, and the sharp little gasp that escaped on a half-squeak made him smile. "It's what friends do."

"You smell like maple syrup, Eli."

"Is this why you can't figure your shit out to take care of our son? You're too busy fucking this guy?"

Elliott winced, and Clare jumped back from him as though she'd been electrocuted.

"What? No. I got stuck in work. Like. I. Told. You." She folded her arms once again. Shields up. "What are you doing here? I told you I worked things out and could pick him up."

"If you'd done that do you think I'd be here?"

Man, this guy was a fucking jerk.

"I texted you." Clare pawed at her bag before producing her phone. She unlocked it, and a flicker of uncertainty passed across her face. She turned the phone to face Douche Bag Dad, her cheeks turning red. "I guess I didn't hit send."

"Idiot."

Nope. Elliott was *not* letting that fly. Stepping toward Fuckface Father, he extended his hand. "Elliott."

Peckerhead Patriarch observed his outstretched arm as though Elliott had offered him an STD.

"I'm a friend of Clare's." Elliott didn't miss her flinch and the disappointment that passed across her face before she settled into indifference. Did she want more between them like he did? Would she have let him kiss her if Sir Shithead Sire hadn't interrupted them?

A flutter in his chest at the thought was overshadowed by Bastard Begetter's frown. What the hell was this guy's deal?

"I really think you should watch your tone right now. She made a mistake. We've all done it. Name calling won't help anything right now." There. That was civil, polite, and way more than the asshole deserved. It wasn't anywhere near the broken nose Elliott ached to bestow on him.

"I can't believe you made me come all the way here when you're already here." The douche canoe ignored Elliott completely and kept talking at Clare.

She frowned but remained quiet. Was this how he always spoke to her?

"She already said it was an accident. It's no big deal, right?" He lowered his voice and curled his fingers tight, blood bubbling under his skin. "No point in making a scene in front of the kids." He jerked his head at the trail of young players coming toward them.

"Dad!" Mason bounded up and threw his arms around the Sperm Donor. "What are you doing here?"

With a wide grin, the man gave Mason a squeeze. "I figured we could have milkshakes. I know you missed out the other night and I thought I'd stop by and take you out for a treat."

The kid's eyes popped wide, sparkling, and while Clare's eyes also doubled in size, it wasn't with the same juvenile excitement as her son.

"But it's a school night. Mom—"

"Mom won't mind. It's just this once, right? It's not like we do it every night." He mussed up Mason's hair.

"Is that true, Mom? Is it really okay?" The hope in Mason's voice only served to fuel the anger simmering in Elliott's stomach. That fucking asshole was playing both Mason *and* Clare like a five-dollar banjo.

She eventually surrendered with a blink and levied a glare at her ex-husband. "Just this once," she spat through gritted teeth and a fake smile.

He didn't blame her, he wouldn't have wanted to cause a scene—or rather, another scene with Mason—at the rink either. But it was more than that. Her fragile smile barely concealed her pain. She was obviously bad cop to Mason's dad's good cop. She was all out of fight.

Deadbeat Dad had the nerve to widen his smug grin and shrug. Elliott flexed his fingers and clenched his fist tighter against his thigh. He'd have given almost anything to wipe the conceited smirk from his face, but that wouldn't help anything either.

Mason hurried off to the locker room, with his prick of a father close on his heels. Elliott had to hand it to him—he excelled at fucking with Clare and hauling ass so she couldn't unleash her anger at him.

Her eyes burned into his back like hot coals as he walked away. Elliott opened his mouth, not sure what he was going to say but feeling the need to say *something*. She shook her head and pointed to the door. He followed her in silence. Waves of rage radiated from her pores as she marched toward the exit.

Once outside, she braced her ass against the side of the rink and bent over, palms on her knees. Her hair fell forward to hide her face. With her hands clutched into balls of rage, she leaned on her forearms and the scream that ripped from her into the evening air was primal, raw, and charged with a pain that had him welling up.

When she stood straight, her head lolled back against the wall of the building. Her bottom lip trembled as her teeth sank into it, and her eyes clouded over as she blinked slowly. He wanted to lay into the douche bag for upsetting her so much. She was unravelling before his eyes and he was helpless to stop it.

Stepping forward, he cupped her face with both hands, sweeping his thumb across the apple of her cheek and wiping away the tears that trickled down her face. The hell if he was letting that piece of shit break her.

CHAPTER 8
Clare

Chest heaving, Clare leaned into the warmth of Elliott's palm and closed her eyes, forcing another surge of tears to escape down her cheeks and onto his hands. She detested that her bastard ex-husband still pushed her buttons like that, and worse still, she despised that Eli had witnessed the whole thing.

Dammit.

Elliott's anger pulsed from his skin, blistering, tangible. His nostrils flared, and his frown was so severe, she was convinced he'd made new wrinkles in his forehead.

It was so fucking hot.

She couldn't remember the last time someone stepped up to bat *for* her, rather than against. Hell, most days it felt like she was being beaten by the damned bat.

Sure, he couldn't help her out when she needed him.

Sure, he snapped her head off and hung up on her earlier.

And sure, he'd reduced them to "just friends" to Alex, Mason's dad, when their history was far more than that, but he'd also defended her.

His presence had been reassuring, encouraging against the

dick she'd stupidly married and had Mason with. While she didn't regret Mason for a second, Alex... Ugh. She wished he was half the man Mason was growing up to be—when he wasn't losing his shit and saying he hated her anyway.

She hadn't been at all embarrassed or ashamed that she'd almost kissed Elliott when the douchebag had interrupted them. In fact, she'd been mad he'd stepped in on their moment. Asshole.

Elliott swept his thumbs across her cheeks again, and she breathed him in. Or tried to. Her snotty nose made it impossible, but she imagined that his fresh pine scent met her nose. Pine with hints of musk, bergamot, and maple fucking syrup. Ugh. It curled around the fire blazing inside her body and lessened the raging storm whipping up a frenzy in her mind.

Her heart skittered. His face was so damn close to hers but he just stared at her, his features unreadable. What was he thinking? Did he want to kiss her? Why *wasn't* he kissing her? Was he waiting for her to make the first move?

Ha. He'd be waiting a long time. Considering how he fucked off, left her alone, and never came back, she was going to make sure he wanted to kiss her before she even considered being the first one to blink.

Except his lips looked so soft, full, and inviting. And he was so goddamn close. If she stuck her tongue out she'd probably reach his plush, Cupid's bow lips.

"He owes you an apology."

She snorted. "That sorry excuse for a person has never apologized to anyone a day in his life." It was easy to make an ex the villain. It gave her somewhere to direct her ire. He wasn't always an asshole, though, she had loved him once, it was why she married him. She sighed. She'd just not been enough to keep him from straying.

Elliot's hazel eyes flared wide, the light catching the gold flecks around his left pupil, but he stayed silent. He trailed his thumb across her bottom lip, sending shivers skating across her skin. They'd kissed in high school, fooled around a bit, but when he'd left she'd let resentment and hate build a home where her love and desire for him had lived.

"Open your eyes, Clare."

She hadn't realized she'd closed them, but her eyelids fluttered open at his request. He sighed. Was he swooning? It totally sounded like a swoon. Was he just going to stand there staring at her? Fuck, did she have something in her teeth?

Oh Christ, did her breath smell like the pickled beets she'd had with her salad for dinner?

"Shhhh." Another sweep of his thumb across her lip. Was he shushing her chaotic brain? Could he hear her frantic thoughts?

Maybe he was shushing her heart. It was making so much noise in her chest he had to have heard it. It wasn't even beating in a delightful rhythm either—it was thrashing around like a toddler trying to avoid putting clothes on.

Even if he had no plans to kiss her, he was distracting her from her asshole ex enough that her blood pressure would be normal if it hadn't been for the fact Elliott was licking his lips and angling his head.

She didn't move. She didn't breathe. She didn't even dare hope—in case she was misreading the situation entirely.

He lowered his lips to hers and barely grazed her skin. Jesus Christ the anticipation was going to kill her. Fighting the urge to grab his shirt and feast on his lips like a woman starved, she somehow channeled patience and waited.

He pulled back just enough to rake his gaze over her face. Was he searching for permission? Her interest?

Couldn't he tell that she was only too fucking eager to have his tongue in her mouth? Or any other part of her body, for that matter. Wasn't it written across her face?

"It's been so long, Ceecee." His voice was pained,

tormented, like he'd experienced the same anguish she had. "I've missed you so much." Another brush of his lips against hers, but this time, she pressed back against him more firmly. It was as though her permission released something inside him.

Pushing her against the wall with his body, he slid a hand around the side of her neck and kissed her, for real. Thank the fucking gods and goddesses. All of them.

Choirs of angels sang, the stars aligned, and every other fucking romantic stereotype from throughout the ages happened all at once. A chain reaction of joy and lust ignited within her body, and her lips parted on a sigh as she blindly grasped for his shirt to tug him closer. Elliott was still her happy place.

His body was unyielding against hers, their tongues colliding with a hunger that left her breathless. Snaking her hand up his chest and threading it around his neck she lost herself in him, giving herself over to the kiss that should have happened all those years ago when he came back from playing hockey.

The kiss that if it *had* happened all those years ago, he never would have left. Or if he'd left, he'd have come back. He would have had to. No one else could have kissed him the way she was. She was sure of it.

It was the kiss to compare all other kisses to. Hell, she never wanted to leave. She never wanted anyone else to kiss him. And she wanted to kiss him forever if every kiss was going to be like this one.

Soft, gentle, yet somehow hungry and commanding. The kind of kiss that told you everything without saying a word. The kind of kiss that made you weak at the knees, breathless, and energized all at once.

His tongue danced with hers, and when it wasn't, he nipped and sucked on her lips like they belonged to him. Like they'd always belonged to him. Her nipples strained against her bra, and she clung to him like she needed him braced against her to survive. Maybe she did.

His hands glided down to her waist, grazing her breasts as they roamed, eliciting a moan from her. She was soaking. She'd never been able to feel how wet she was from just a kiss before. And his erection was hard to miss considering it was pressed against her body. Fuck. He was rock hard. For her.

From just one kiss.

Was this what it was supposed to be like when someone kissed you? She felt cheated. Cat's dad kissed like an open mouthed fish, and Alex... Well, he barely ever kissed her at all. She'd never really questioned that she was missing out until right now, this moment, until Elliott kissed her like it was his entire life's purpose.

He kissed her like the secret to eternal life lay in her mouth and he was determined to search every square inch of it until he found it. She sighed, sagging against his firm body as she clawed at the hair at his nape and deepened their kiss.

When he pulled back, cold air swirled where his warmth had been. She frowned and her body protested his absence. She wasn't done kissing him. Why had he stopped? Didn't it rock his world like it had hers? Her fingers drifted to her lips as she examined his face.

His chest rose and fell with obvious effort as he shook his head. "I can't keep kissing you out here. If I do, there's a real chance your ex and your son will see you in a state of semi-nakedness while I fuck you senseless all the way to tomorrow."

Holy. Fuck. Her pulse thumped at the base of her neck while pure unadulterated need throbbed between her thighs.

Neither of her exes were dirty talkers. But if Elliott kept telling her what he was going to do to her, she was going to orgasm where she stood. Clamping her knees together, she rolled her lips between her teeth and nodded. If she was honest with herself, there was a piece of her that didn't even care.

Elliott's phone rang, and his face fell. "I have to." Agony swirled in his hazel depths. "With Mom... I..." He pulled his phone from his back pocket and the color drained from his face. "It's her assisted living facility." He was already pressing the screen to answer the call.

She hugged herself, suddenly cold and worried. When they were kids, Elliott's mom had been so laid back and cool. She never let them do anything particularly wild, but she always gave them enough independence that Clare had never felt overly restricted.

Elliott listened quietly before nodding. "I'll be right there." He brushed his fingers along her jaw. "I need to go. Mom fell in the bathroom and needs sutures. She lost her shit at them and they had to sedate her. They think it might help if I'm there when she wakes up. They're on their way to the hospital now."

Clare picked up her discarded purse from the ground next to their feet. "I'll drive."

"I can't ask you to do that, Clare."

"Well, it's a good thing I offered then, isn't it? Let's go." She shot off a text to Mason's dad to tell him where she was going. He'd be pissed, but considering he had just undermined her in front of their son, she didn't give a shit. Fuck him.

If he wanted to villainize her for being a good person, for helping a friend, then let him. But Elliott's hands were trembling, and he still looked as pale as a sheet. She wasn't letting him drive anywhere.

"I'm not repeating myself, Eli-Belly. Get in the car."

He snorted. "Not if you're going to dredge up that *beloved* nickname."

Clare flicked her hair over her shoulder. "She wuuuved

you, Eli-Belly. She called her Ken doll Elliott and made kissy noises for Christ's sake."

Elliott's mom had told her about the girl next door who had such a crush on Elliott when they were little that she turned into something of a pint-sized stalker at only eight years old. Mrs. S. had told Clare that they'd come home and find this Elliott-obsessed little girl sitting at their dining table playing house with Elliott-Ken and Barbie.

He shuddered. "I wonder where she is now."

"Probably in your house smelling your boxers." Clare shrugged, unlocked the car, and jerked a thumb at it. "Which hospital?"

"Mercy. And I get to DJ."

She arched a brow at him, over the top of the car as she opened the door. "You drive a hard bargain."

They made it to the hospital in minutes.

"You okay?" she asked as she pulled into a parking space. Elliott's complexion had changed from pasty white to a gonna-puke green.

"You're never driving again. Not just me. I mean anyone, ever."

She laughed. "I have to take you back to your car."

"I'll walk." He clutched his stomach. "How the hell do you still have your license? Wait, how are you even still alive? You know a red light isn't a suggestion, right?"

"It wasn't red. It was yellow."

His forehead wrinkled as his brow shot up. "Are you color blind? Is that what the problem is? Christ." He stepped out of the car and rubbed his temples. "You are a terrible driver, Clare Reynolds."

She laughed harder and shook her head. He wasn't the first person to say that to her. "I've survived this long, haven't I?"

"That's your bar? Surviving?"

"My grandma was one of those fearful old lady drivers who always went ten under the speed limit. She used to boast that she'd never been in an accident and my dad would always say under his breath, "But you cause them every time you get behind the wheel."" She shrugged. "I guess I went a little the other way."

His brows shot up when she said a little, but he said nothing.

She motioned to the door to the hospital. "Want me to go with you? I can stay here. I don't mind."

His head snapped back and forth between the hospital and the car. "Would you mind waiting here? I don't know that she'll remember you. If she doesn't, she might get stressed, or there could be two hundred questions that add to her frustration, and mine. I just..." He shrugged. "I never know what I'm going to get with her anymore."

Ignoring the spikes of disappointment and pain jabbing at her stomach, she nodded. It wasn't about her, and all things considered, she had no right to be upset. It wasn't that he didn't need her, or want her, it was about him and his unwell mom. It was that simple.

"I can take an Uber or a Lyft back to the rink for my car if you'd like to go home. I don't want to cause any more hassle for you than I already have."

She tossed him a smile. "It's what friends are for, Eli. I'll be here when you're done." She waved her phone at him. "I've got a date with my smut."

He pointed at her. "This conversation isn't over." With a clear sadness she felt in her bones, he turned and jogged into the building.

An hour later, her cell phone rang jolting her out of an unplanned nap. "Mase-Mallow? What's wrong?"

"Nothing, Mom. I just wanted to let you know that Dad dropped me off at home and Cat's here. We're good."

"Okay. Thanks, kiddo. I'll be home as soon as I can." She spoke through a yawn, sensing hesitation through the line. "Mason? What is it?"

"It's just..." He cleared his throat. "Dad said you're dating Coach Swift. Is it true? Are you?"

She bit into her fist to stop her from groaning or swearing out loud. She didn't want to lie to her son, she didn't want to put him in the position of being caught in the middle between her and his dad, or being pressured to pass information to him. But there also wasn't much to tell. They weren't really dating, were they?

Sighing, she cursed Alex in her mind and opted for being as transparent as she could. "That wasn't really your dad's place to share, Mason. I'm sorry you didn't hear it directly from me, I promise I wasn't keeping anything from you."

She rubbed the bridge of her nose with her thumb and forefinger. "Elliott and I are old friends. We aren't dating."

"But you'd like to?" Was that hope in the kid's voice?

"I think so. I mean, it obviously depends on what he wants, too, but yes, I'd like to see where things go with him. Would that be okay with you?"

"Totally." He took a drink of something and sighed. "It would make it easier for me to go live with Dad if you weren't alone."

Knife to heart. Vital organs compromised. Instant oxygen deprivation. He still wanted to leave? He'd mentioned it months ago but she'd thought they'd put that to bed. Things were better. They were happy—or so she thought.

Her stomach heaved. She couldn't throw up in her car. Closing her eyes for a moment, she steadied her breath. What other burdens were her too-young-for-this-drama child carrying that she didn't know about?

Tears pricked in her eyes and her whole body shook, with

the cold, with tiredness, and with a soul-deep agony. If Mason moved in with that asshat, she'd barely ever see him.

Every other weekend and rotating holidays. That's what she'd get. It wouldn't be enough. Not with Catriona going off to college and moving out of the house.

The idea of living in an empty house crashed into her like a freight train. Not to mention the fact her son didn't want to live with her anymore. Was she really that bad?

She'd have to get a cat. Or ten cats. That's what she'd do. She'd fill the gaping void in her chest, in her life, with feline companions who looked down their noses at her like her kids did. Cats who turned their noses up at their food like her kids did, and who sprawled out and took up every inch of space—just like her kids did. It would be like they never left. Yes, that was what she'd do.

"Mom?"

"We can talk about it tomorrow when I'm home, okay?"

"Sure, Mom." Another long pause. "And Mom?"

"Yeah?" A shiver rattled through her and she wished she'd put her coat back into the trunk of the car after she'd washed a ketchup catastrophe off it.

"Tell Coach Swift I hope his mom gets better soon."

Emotion clogged her throat, and her heart splintered into a bazillion pieces at his sweet nature. "I will."

He hung up and left her staring at her screen. A picture of Clare and both kids from over a year ago, she'd have to update it if they were both moving out. Cat had matured so much since the picture, and Mason had shot up so he was taller than both of them.

Another jolt of pain in her chest. Fuck. Was she such a bad mother that he couldn't bear to live with her?

A knock on the window made her shriek. Clutching at her chest she acknowledged Elliott's wave through the glass and unlocked the doors.

"Sorry." He slipped into the passenger side and buckled his seatbelt. "I did try to be obvious about my approach, but you were in a world of your own."

She forced a smile, her heart still smarting at Mason's announcement that he wanted to move in with Alex. "You're lucky I opted for the screaming, rather than the self-defense. I could have killed you." She wagged her finger at him. "I'm a highly trained assassin." At his unsmiling face, she sobered. "How is she?"

His beautiful features darkened even more, and he aged a decade right in front of her eyes. "Pretty beat up. Like I said, she slipped in the bathroom but they said she wouldn't let anyone help her. She needed a shit ton of stitches, some wicked nasty bruising, and an attitude to boot. She thought I was dad, gave me shit about leaving her with incompetent assholes who wouldn't even let her shower alone."

"Did you correct her? Tell her who you were?"

He shook his head. "When she's that worked up it makes no difference. Path of least resistance is sometimes the easiest for everyone." He raked his palms over his face and through his hair. Tipping his head back made the street light reflect off the tears pooling in his eyes. "It's a fucker of a disease. Some days, she's fine. She remembers who I am, and every detail of our lives with startling accuracy. Others, she thinks it's decades ago, that I'm Dad, or worse... she doesn't remember me at all."

His voice cracked, and while she wanted to envelop him in her arms and not let anything else upset him, he was fading fast. She needed to get him home so he could collapse into bed and hopefully sleep through some of his grief.

She started the car and squeezed his hand. "Let's get you home." She had nothing else to offer, no words of wisdom, no magic cure. He was right. Alzheimer's was a bastard of a disease, one she knew very little about.

But one thing she did know was that nothing she said or

did could cure either his mom of her illness or take away his pain. It wasn't something one of her many mom lists could fix, and she hated it.

They drove through McDonalds on the way home to get him a cheeseburger and fries to quiet his growling stomach. As she sipped on her milkshake on the way from his house to hers, she wondered if she even had the mental energy she'd need to pursue something personal, something intimate with him.

He had a lot going on, and so did she. She was already low on mental spoons, and fuck, she barely had enough strength to bathe and feed herself, never mind help take care of another grown-ass adult. But, as she pulled into her driveway and slurped at the final mouthfuls of strawberry deliciousness, she wondered if she would ever be able to forgive herself for not taking a shot with Elliott if he was interested too.

Sure, things would be hard, but her life without him had been even harder. And her stomach hurt at the thought of going back there. She owed it to herself to shoot her shot, right? Second chances didn't come around every day. She needed to grab it with both hands and see where it took her.

CHAPTER 9
Elliott

"Coach Swift, what was your strategy to ensure the Snow Pirates' sheer domination in the third period?"

Standing in the corridor outside the locker room in Madison, Wisconsin, post-game, Elliott had no idea who this guy asking questions was. In all the years he'd been playing at their barn, he'd never met this kid before.

He had a lanyard around his neck and frantically scribbled on a notebook, so a reporter, sure, but for who? The university?

And why were they suddenly taking an interest in him? In the Snow Pirates? Or were they now interviewing the coach of every visiting team? Elliott had questions. But didn't care enough to actually ask any of them.

The young guy paused, lifted the nib of his pen from the paper and canted his head. "Coach?"

Oh. Yes. He needed to actually answer the kid's question. Clearing his throat he bought himself an extra second or two to mull on the question. "I think one of the hardest—yet most important—things in hockey is to recognize when you're getting outplayed and outcoached. I think my refusal to make line changes and in-game adjustments for the first two periods almost cost us the game."

The kid's mouth dropped open, like he wasn't expecting Elliott to own his mistakes.

He heaved out a sigh. "It was inexcusable, really."

The reporter scribbled like his life depended on it, his brows high and eyes wide.

"It was clear the forward lines weren't working, and I should have changed them sooner. It was almost too late. Doing the same thing over and over and expecting different results isn't going to work. It's a rookie mistake. I think I just needed to get out of my own head and trust my gut."

The man nodded. "You're saying you had way too many passengers up front?"

Elliott arched a brow. "That's not what I'm saying at all. I stand by my team. They did what I asked of them. I'm saying the buck stops with me. I'm the guy calling the plays, and I should have switched it up earlier in the game. Not to mention, any other team who went down by three so quickly would have folded the tents."

The pen continued to move at speed across the paper as the kid snorted. "I'll say. Not your Snow Pirates though. They didn't quit." He paused and tapped the pen on his chin. "I can't recall a time when I've seen such heart on the ice that wasn't a playoff game. They left it all out there. Those special teams are impressive."

The awe in his voice made Elliott puff out his chest. Damn straight his boys were impressive. He nodded. "We have great coaches working hard with the guys, and some exceptional talent on the roster. It's shaping up to be an excellent season."

The reporter gnawed on the end of his pen. Elliott wanted to snatch it from his hand and thwap him on the nose with the damn thing.

"I really thought y'all'd suffer with Mo, Obi, and Morgan graduating and moving on." He murmured it as though he was talking more to himself than to Elliott, but he couldn't fault the assumption. The trio of seniors leaving had hit the team hard, but thankfully there was still plenty of talent and heart left to more than pick up the slack. He just needed to utilize their skills in the right way.

The kid flicked his pen against the notebook and tucked it into his back pocket. "Thanks for taking the time to talk to me, Coach. My readers love when I go a little further with the visiting teams." He produced a card. "If you want to read it, or..." He shrugged and rubbed at the back of his neck, his face turning pink in the corridor. "Feel like commenting on the interview on our social pages... That'd be cool."

Elliott tucked the business card into his wallet and nodded. "I'll do that. Thanks for the interview."

The kid's face lit up like the Empire State Building and his head threatened to fall from his body as he nodded and walked away. "Oh!" His shoes squeaked on the floor as he turned back to Elliott. "If you like Italian food, try Nonno's. Best in town." He flicked a wave and left.

Italian it was. As he waited for the team to get their shit sorted and get to the bus to go the hotel for the night, he pulled up the menu for Giulia back in Minnesota. It was a double header weekend, so they were in Madison for the duration, but that didn't mean he and Clare couldn't have a virtual date.

Before he ordered food for her, he needed to double check she was still going to be home. It had been two weeks since their first kiss. Their *only* kiss. They hadn't managed to steal any alone time to repeat it, or do anything else for that matter.

And fuck he wanted to bury himself between her thighs and make her tremble and whimper his name. Once he got back from Wisconsin, he would be home for a while, and he was determined to turn that first kiss into more of a habit. Then he'd make her come undone on his dick.

Her soft, plush lips pressed against his tortured his dreams still. He wanted to repeat it. He needed to repeat it. And then some.

> Elliott: Are you still staying home tonight? Nothing's changed?

> Clare: Why? You magically back early and want to hang out?

> Elliott: I wish. I'm going to guess you haven't had dinner. Wanna eat together?

> Clare: Correct assumption. I've been buried under a pile of laundry today and attempting to get the house in order. What did you have in mind?

> Elliott: I'm about to head back to the hotel. Wanna pick a movie for us to watch together and I'll take care of dinner?

> Clare: You really want to let me pick the movie?

> Elliott: I'd rather you picked a shit movie than used 'eenie, meenie, miny, mo' to find my dinner. I'm too fucking hungry to risk a dubious meal. I got a rec from a local and I already know where to get yours.

> Clare: Sounds good to me.

> Clare: Oh, hey. Shit.

> Elliott: ????

> Clare: Great game, Coach!

He couldn't stop the smile from splitting his face.

"You okay, Coach?" Linc tossed his equipment bag into the open belly of the bus and walked toward him. "There's a weird thing going on with your face."

"Holy shit, is he...smiling?" Russ smacked Linc's chest as he dumped his duffel, too.

"Do we need to call someone, Coach?" Linc reached a hand toward Elliott's forehead. "Do you have a fever?"

"Someone needs to check that hell hasn't frozen over, man. This is pretty serious."

Linc paused at the bottom of the steps to the bus. "I don't think that grin is because of our epic comeback on the ice tonight, Russell. That grin is for a woman." He shook his head slowly as though it were a terminal affliction. "Coach, is there a chance you're wooing a lady?"

Russ snorted. "No one says wooing anymore, Linc. You need to get your head out of those historical romances you're buddy reading with Cleo, man."

Shrugging, Linc wagged a finger at his friend. "I won't let you smut shame me, Russell Stewart."

Russ chuckled. "Is it true, Coach? Is this..." He waved a hand at Elliott's face. "Is this because of...?" He dropped his voice to a theatrical whisper. "A woman?"

Linc sang "dun, dun, duuuuuun" before dissolving into laughter.

Elliott couldn't help but laugh with them, talking to Clare had brought a levity back into his life he hadn't felt for so long. It wasn't surprising his guys were picking up on it.

"In fairness, he's been less...y'know...for a while now." Linc looked everywhere but at Elliott.

Elliott folded his arms. "Less what, Lincoln?"

Linc held his hands up. "You know..." The kid's face was starting to sizzle.

Russ shoved Linc's shoulder. "Idiot. Stop talking before

you end up skating your legs off doing laps at practice. What he means to say is, he's glad to see you happy, Coach. Whoever she is, just don't fuck it up. We have enough going on with Will and his woman right now."

How the hell could he fuck it up when he hadn't even gotten whatever *it* was with Clare off the fucking ground? It was easy not to fuck something up when you couldn't see each other. He couldn't wait to see her. He was almost embarrassed by the flutter in his stomach, but that kiss had invaded his dreams every night for the past two weeks, and he ached to repeat it.

Linc pointed a finger at Elliott's lips. "There it is again. She must be something special."

"Are you taking her to prom?" Russ waggled his eyebrows. Will Morrison had masterminded a prom night as both a fundraiser for a local charity *Pippa's Place* as well as a grand gesture to win back his girl. It gave everyone in the Snow Pirate's circle an excuse to glam up and let their hair down for an evening. It felt like it was all anyone was talking about.

"If she says yes." He shrugged. "Get your asses on the bus. *She's* waiting for dinner."

The two players whooped and hooted. "Atta boy, Coach. Virtual date. Romantic. I didn't know you were the romantic type, Coach. I like it." Linc nodded approvingly. "Are you sending her dinner?"

Elliott gave an almost imperceptible nod as the rest of the team pushed past the three of them and clambered into the bus.

Linc winked and cocked two finger guns. "Send her dessert."

He hadn't thought to send something sweet. But on the ride back to the hotel he ordered food for them, including dessert and picked up a couple of beers from the bar on the way up to his room.

Even with his chipper mood, his players knew better than to fuck around with curfew, but he checked and double checked that they were all in their rooms before taking his food from the DoorDash delivery guy and retreating to his room.

> Clare: You sent a lot of food.

>> Elliott: What you mean to say is: thank you Eli.

> Clare: No. What I mean to say is: you sent a lot of food.

> Clare: Also, thank you.

>> Elliott: You're welcome. I wasn't sure if you had Mase and Cat this weekend, or if they had other plans. I didn't want to leave them out.

> Clare: You totally knew I was alone.

>> Elliott: Okay, fine. I figured sending enough to have leftovers for lunch tomorrow wouldn't be the worst thing in the world.

> Clare: Accurate on all counts.

> Clare: Fuck. This chicken parm is making me moan more than my Ravishing Rose Clit Pleaser.

Elliott sprayed the tiny office table with a thin film of beer, inhaled bubbly liquid particles, and coughed until his eyes watered.

> Clare: So fucking good. How's your Alfredo?

> Elliott: Two secs. Still recovering from the casual vibrator drop.

> Elliott: Ravishing rose clit pleaser? Do share with the rest of the class.

> Clare: Oh please. Like you didn't know I had a collection.

A collection?

> Elliott: I'm an old man, Ceecee. My heart can't take this excitement. Are you trying to kill me?

He cleared his throat with a few gulps of beer.

> Clare: I've been single for a long time. You didn't think I had bedroom assistance?

> Clare: My arm would have fallen off long ago, for Christ's sake!!!!

> Clare: Okay. That makes it sound like I'm some kind of sex fiend.

> Clare: I don't have a problem. I'm just exhausted by the end of the day and can't be bothered with the DIY, y'know?

> Clare: I'm efficient. Yup. That's what I am.

He couldn't help but laugh.

> Clare: You're laughing at me right now, aren't you?

His dick certainly wasn't laughing. His quickly cooling down food wasn't even keeping his attention as all he could think about was Clare lying spread out in her bed pleasuring herself. It was enough to make his mouth dry up.

> Elliott: I can't say I'm laughing, no.

> Elliott: And to circle back a little, the Alfredo was delicious, but I lost interest as soon as you started talking about your pussy. I'm sure it's much more delicious. I'd much rather feast on that.

Clare: Do you kiss your momma with that mouth, Mr. Swift?

Clare: Okay, I take that back. I made it weird by bringing up your mom during a sexy time text, didn't I? Sorry.

Elliott laughed again.

> Elliott: Little bit, yeah.

Clare: Can you tell it's been a while since I've flirted with anyone?

> Elliott: It has? But you're so skilled at it.

Clare: I hate you.

> Elliott: Liar.

Clare: This is why I have toys, my clit pleaser doesn't get sassy with me.

> Elliott: Because it's ravishing?

Clare: You really wanna feast on my pussy?

> Elliott: Oh, only for a couple decades or so. The idea of you using toys for so long is fucking criminal, Clare. I want to take care of you.

He wasn't lying. His fingers ached to tug on her nipples while his tongue circled her clit. Food forgotten, he moved to the side of the bed and stripped before sliding between the sheets.

> Elliott: Where are you?

> Clare: Pass.

He grinned.

> Elliott: No passing. Where are you, Clare?

> Clare: Would you believe me if I told you I was on the couch with what's left of my chicken parm?

> Elliott: Not when I'm lying in my bed with my rock hard cock in my hand, no. I wouldn't.

She didn't reply for a long minute, and the sinking feeling in his stomach suggested he'd fucked up, that he'd misread her desire, or overplayed his hand. Shit. Was he going to lose her all over again because he was a horny fucker?

His grip on his shaft loosened as the dots informing him she was typing moved on the screen. His chest stayed tight until a picture of her in black lace underwear appeared. He swallowed hard. She was fucking magnificent.

> Elliott: I know lace underwear is expensive AF. But if I promise to buy you a new pair can I rip those panties off you? Please and thank you.

> Clare: You really like it?

> Elliott: You can't be serious right now.

> Elliott: It's not the underwear I like, Ceecee.

A bead of precum seeped from his slit and slipped down the head of his cock.

> Elliott: If it wasn't ungentlemanly, I'd show you just how hard my cock is for you right now, Clare Reynolds.

Her hand covered her stomach in the picture. As though she was self-conscious, or ashamed of her tummy.

> Elliott: What are you trying to hide with that arm across your middle?

> Clare: My body and I aren't exactly on the best of terms right now. Even taking that picture is a big deal for me, never mind actually sending it. I almost didn't.

So that had been what the pregnant pause was all about, not her indecision with him, but with herself. Her vulnerability soaked through the screen and shot into his chest. What he wouldn't give to pull her against his chest and tell her a million times that she'd always been the most beautiful girl in the world to him.

He'd contemplated asking her for a video call, but knowing how in her head she was about her body, he didn't want to make her feel any more uncomfortable than she already did.

> Elliott: I'm glad you did. I don't know how you're so clueless about your beauty, but you are breathtaking.

> Elliott: And for the record… I don't just mean breathtaking with clean and shiny hair, red lips, and sexy black lace underwear. You're breathtaking, period. With your messy top knot, fuck the patriarchy tees, and your crazy patterned yoga pants.

> Clare: Making me cry, Eli. And for a good reason this time.

Ow. The shards of guilt and regret lodged in his heart sank a little deeper.

> Elliott: Total MILF. Better?

> Clare: LOL!!

> Clare: My arm is attempting to hide my C-section scar from Mason. I love the kid but goddammit if he wasn't a chunky, stubborn baby. Emergency C-section at damn near 49 weeks.

> Clare: Okay, it wasn't 49 weeks, not even close but I can tell you, it sure as shit felt like it was.

> Elliott: You never need to hide any pieces of yourself from me, Clare.

> Clare: Keep talking. Pretty sure a combination of your filthy mouth and your touching sweetness is gonna bag me a screaming O without using any of these toys I have next to me on my bed.

His dick twitched, reminding him that it was still there, still rock hard, weeping and aching for release. He curled his fingers around the base and pumped twice, long, languid strokes. He wished he could reach through the phone and trace his fingers along the scalloped black lace on her tits.

He wanted to worship at the Temple of Clare, to make her soaking wet and desperate with need before making her come so intensely, and so often, that she couldn't remember her ex's names. Then he wanted to fuck her so hard, she forgot her own.

> Clare: Wanna pick which toy I should play with?

She sent him a picture of the vibrators and toys next to her on the bed. It looked like some strange perp line up, and he got to pick the one who did it—or rather, would do it. He chuckled at how open she was about her toys, if only he could get her to be so at ease with her body, too.

> Elliott: Is that a glass… tentacle?

> Clare: I like the bumps.

> Elliott: Is that a fist?

> Clare: I like feeling full.

He liked that she wasn't defensive, or trying to deflect. She was simply telling him what she liked about each of the toys.

> Elliott: What's the thing with three… parts?

> Clare: That's my tri-brator, for when I'm feeling a lil kinky and want something in my butt.

A little kinky. Clare Reynolds. Kinky. In the name of all that was holy, how was this his life? His sweet and innocent best friend from childhood had a sex toy collection that only wet dreams were made of.

> Clare: You better not be judging me Elliott Swift.

> Elliott: I'd never dream of it. I'm distracted by that snail looking thing. What's that?

> Clare: It's my snail vibe. The concept is actually kinda genius. The trouble with most rabbit vibrators is that the two arms don't always align… uh… where I need them to. This thing? Well. The clit stimulator unfurls as you insert the toy. No matter how deep you insert that nub on the far left, the curly vibe on top will always be resting on your clit.

> Clare: My clit.

> Elliott: Fuck.

He wanted her clit between his fucking teeth so he could flick it with the tip of his tongue and make her mewl.

> Elliott: I want that pink swirly unicorn horn inside you now.

> Clare: Ah. Ah. Ah. I wants don't get.

> Elliott: I'm about three minutes from blowing my load all over those creamy tits of yours on my screen. I need it inside you. Now.

> Clare: Say please.

> Elliott: I'm trying so hard not to embarrass myself right now. Please hurry up, Clare.

He gritted his teeth and hissed as the pressure grew in his balls. Another picture appeared on his screen, this one was of her pussy, and the glass unicorn horn buried all the way inside her.

The familiar tingle of release prickled at the base of his spine as he tightened his grip on his cock.

> Elliott: Such a pretty pussy. Circle that clit for me.

Clare: Pick a toy.

> Elliott: The purple suction one. And you'd better enjoy everything it has to offer, because once I'm back in town you're coming on my fucking tongue.

Clare: I'm close, Elliott.

He grunted with effort at holding back his own release.

> Elliott: Don't

> Elliott: Stop

He should have called her. Typing with one hand while trying to fist fuck your own dick was awkward AF.

Clare's name lit up the screen and he smashed his thumb against the "answer" button. No video, but he could at least get to hear her and he wouldn't have to type, either. Her little pants and moans as she crested towards her orgasm made him bite into his lip to try to draw out his own climax.

"Come for me, Clare. Make your pretty little pussy come for me."

A muffled "fuck," a change in the pitch of the buzzing, and a drawn out moan had him fisting his cock with jerky, frustrated movements. He should be there, between her thighs, buried deep in her soaking wet tight pussy, drilling her while she screamed his name and cried out for deities.

"I'm gonna…" Two pants, then she screamed.

He chased her over the edge. Jets of warm cum sprayed over his stomach as he grunted through his release.

"Fuck."

He nodded, forgetting for a second that she couldn't see him. "I can't wait to get back home so I can fuck you, Clare."

Something brushed against the speaker on her end. "I never thought I'd be a lover of a filthy tongue, but I gotta say, Eli… You totally did it for me."

"Just wait until I'm wedged between your thighs licking up your delicious juices with my filthy tongue."

"Delicious juices shouldn't sound hot to me. I know it shouldn't."

"And yet?"

She moaned again. "I can't go again." She yawned. "I'm too fucking tired."

He chuckled. "We'll need to work on that too. I imagine once I see your cheeks all flushed from a good fucking I'm going to want to keep them pink."

"Thank you, Elliott."

"Please tell me you aren't thanking me for the orgasm."

"No." Her voice was small. "For not asking to see me on a video call. I was a little self-conscious."

"You don't need to thank me for that, either."

"It was kind of you not to push to see me."

He wiped his sticky hand on the sheet next to him and tucked his palms behind his head. "I have this beautiful picture of you. It was enough for now. I can't wait to get my hands on you."

She yawned and made a humming noise before a thud echoed through the line.

"You okay?"

"Dropped a toy." Her adorable mumble suggested she was heading toward sleep fast. But he hadn't yet asked her the most important question of the night.

"You fading on me, Ceecee?"

"Mmhmm."

"What about your shitty movie?"

"Too sleepy."

He grinned and mentally patted himself on the back. He had no interest in watching a romcom with Katherine Heigl. Score one for the win!

"I have a question."

"You do?" She sounded a little more alert.

"Wanna go to prom with me?"

CHAPTER 10
Clare

"Where is this prom?" Cat cocked a brow, planting both hands on her hips in the doorway to Clare's bedroom. She sat in front of her vanity, carefully applying makeup and hoping that the hot rollers in her hair would be enough to give her the warm, loose curls she was aiming for.

"At Pippa's community center." She swept her eyeshadow applicator across her lid, and at Cat's creased forehead, she continued. "Near the women's shelter. It's a fundraiser."

Catriona waggled her finger at Clare. "I know what happens after prom, Mom. I hope you're careful." She folded her arms. "I probably have a condom in my wallet if you need one."

Clare groaned. "You're really giving me a safe sex talk? I'm literally a walking advertisement for safe sex. I got pregnant the first time I had—"

"Lalalalalalalalalalalaaaaaaaaa!" Catriona jammed her fingers in her ears and smushed her eyes shut.

Clare shrugged. "You started it."

Cat flopped down onto the bed. "What are you wearing?"

She finished the flick of her liquid eyeliner, turning her head to make sure the wing was symmetrical on both sides before jerking her head at the closet. "It's hanging in there. Not sure I'm brave enough though. I have a backup."

Catriona jerked open the door and gasped, stepping back and clutching her chest with both hands. "Mom. This... Wow. This is stunning. Where'd you get it from?"

She wiggled her head from side to side. "Truthfully? From your grandmother. It's an authentic 70's prom dress."

"She wore that to her prom? Holy shit! Trailblazer." She picked up the shimmering gold fabric and let it slide through her hand. "It's so pretty. I'm surprised she was allowed out of the house in that."

"I don't think she was. I think her and some friends changed on the way there."

The gown was a floor length, dazzling gold dress with a mid-thigh split. A simple band across the middle broke up the monotony of the dress, jazzing up the plain fabric, and it had a v-cut bodice with thin straps. She paired it with triple loop gold sandals, and gold accessories.

It was a lot of gold.

"You don't think it's... I dunno...too much? Too young? Too shiny...or something?"

Cat folded her arms and tapped a finger on her chin before nodding. Clare's stomach dropped.

"I think you're too freakin' hard on yourself, Mom. It's perfect."

With a smile, Clare bounced up from her chair and embraced her daughter. "Let's see how it looks on, what do you say?"

Catriona nibbled on her bottom lip.

"What is it? Are you okay?"

"Other than being totally jelly no one asked me to prom?" She worked her lip again. "I'm really happy for you, Mom. I haven't seen you light up like this...well...maybe ever. You deserve to be happy."

A lump sprung into Clare's throat, and she tipped her head back to blink away the tears. "I can't ruin my makeup," she rasped while fanning both her eyes.

"Let's get Cinderella ready for the ball." Cat unzipped the dress, slid it from the hanger, and held it out for Clare to slip into.

The cool fabric made her shiver as it fell to floor with a swish. "You sure I don't look like a walking disco ball?"

"Isn't that kind of the point? The 70's was the disco era, right? And of all the walking disco balls in the world, you're my favorite."

She snorted. "I'm really not sure you're helping much right now, Catriona Reynolds."

With a shrug, Cat reached out and squeezed her hand. "I think you look like a million bucks, Mom. Don't let your inner critic screw you over tonight. Okay? I forbid it."

Stepping forward to cradle her daughter's cheeks, Clare sighed. "When did you get so sensible?"

"Had a pretty good teacher."

The doorbell chimed, and her stomach clenched. She'd known this man since before he could aim correctly in a toilet bowl. Why was she so damned nervous? The tiny voice at the back of her head screamed that he might leave her again and not to let him back into her heart, but they both knew it was already too late. He'd never really left.

Smoothing down her dress she did a small spin for Cat who nodded with a wide grin still stuck on her face. She reached over onto the bed and picked up Clare's gold clutch and handed it to her. "I'll go let him in. You put your shoes on."

Clare nodded and slid her feet into the sandals then pulled out the rollers and floofed and sprayed her hair. With a deep breath, she tucked some lipstick into her purse and took one last look at herself in the mirror. It was too late to change anything, so she headed downstairs.

Elliott waited for her at the bottom of the stairs, and when she got close enough, he whistled through his teeth and stretched out a hand to help her down the last few steps. "You... Wow, Ceecee. You look...wow. Just...stunning."

His wide eyes drifted over her from head to toe, almost caressing her with a stare so intense she wanted to clench her thighs—but didn't want to be too obvious in such a form-fitting dress. When she stepped off the last stair next to him, her face and neck heated.

"You sure? I have a 'Y'all need feminism' shirt fresh out of the laundry that I could pair with some ripped jeans and boots if you'd rather."

He swept his hand across her cheek with a touch so soft it almost brought her to tears. "You'd rock the shit out of that get up, but no, I think you look pretty perfect just as you are." He turned to the little table behind him in the entry way, picked up a box, and handed it to her with a shrug.

"I wanted to do it right."

Her chest warmed as she opened the box and trailed her fingers over the delicate corsage. Tiny cream flowers with a sparkle in the center, pearls and gold leaves finished with cream ribbon bows and set on a pearl elastic bracelet. Delicate, beautiful, and it matched her dress.

Not bad, Swift. Not bad at all.

He slipped it over her hand and placed it on her wrist with an affirming nod.

"You look mighty pleased with yourself, Eli." She brushed at the lapel on his tuxedo jacket to remove some lint.

"It took me an embarrassingly long time to choose that corsage. I'm just glad it goes with your dress."

She couldn't help but laugh at the strained expression on his face.

"Come in here! Let me get a picture of you before you go."

They followed Catriona's voice into the living room where she stood by the fireplace, phone in one hand and Nikon DSLR camera in the other. She must have gotten her creativity from her sperm donor, because the photos she took with even just a cell phone were more breathtakingly beautiful than anything Clare had ever done in her entire life.

"You gonna make us pose like real prom pictures?" She arched a brow at her daughter.

"Damn straight. You remember how OTT you were for my prom? This is my revenge."

Elliott grunted, seemingly to hide the chuckle shaking his body, but Clare wasn't letting him get away with it. "Don't encourage her, Elliott."

He held his hands up. "From where I stand she doesn't need any encouragement."

"Hashtag fact. Now hurry up, stand nice or you'll be late. I need pictures for the album and pictures for the socials." She held up each hand as she spoke.

A grueling fifteen minutes later and Clare was over it. "Let's go."

Catriona nodded as she flicked through the pictures on the screen at the back of her camera with a dreamy sigh. "Look." She turned the camera around and an involuntary squeak escaped Clare. Was that really her?

"Do you believe me now? You look amazing, Mom. I wish I was going to prom." She dropped her camera to her side with another dramatic sigh.

"Actually..." Elliott pinned Clare with a look she couldn't decipher.

"What?" She whispered at him even though Cat was only like a foot away.

Elliott bugged out his eyes. "I don't want to overstep and upset you again."

"You know I can hear you both, right? I didn't accidentally fall under my invisibility cloak again, riiiiight?"

Clare flapped a hand toward her daughter before planting her hands on her hips and jerking her chin at Elliott. "Speak."

"One of the kids on the team isn't from here, a rookie, doesn't know many people, going alone..." He glanced at Cat, and Clare's gaze followed.

Clare tipped her head with an expectant pause.

"Blind date prom? Hell yes!" Cat fist-pumped above her head. "I'll be ready in ten."

Somehow, despite her daughter's penchant for taking forever to get ready, they arrived at the community center early. She'd bet her bottom dollar that Cat dumped half her wardrobe over her floor and bed trying to figure out what to wear. But that was future Clare's problem.

Present Clare couldn't believe the transformation at the building. The hockey team had really pulled out all the stops for such a good cause.

"Clare Reynolds, as I live and breathe." Pippa—of Pippa's Place, the local women's shelter and charity that provided whatever help they could to local women—strode toward her like a Hollywood actress. She wore a cotton candy pink halter gown with a slit all the way up to her mid-thigh. Though Pippa's thigh looked less like the cottage cheese skin Clare was flashing as she walked.

Pippa air kissed both of Clare's cheeks before stepping back to appraise her outfit. "You look fucking delectable. And this beautiful young woman must be your daughter." She stepped forward to Cat and cupped Cat's hand with both her own. "It's so nice to meet you."

Cat beamed. "I'm so excited for prom."

In some moments Catriona Reynolds seemed wise beyond her years and grown too fast, but as the wonder in her eyes and voice carried through the night air, Clare was relieved that she had still held on to some of the magic.

Clare rolled her eyes. "She's excited to meet you too, Pippa. She's heard *all* about how you helped me out through the years."

Cat nodded. "I *am* excited to meet you. I'm just... It's prom, Mom!"

"Hi Pippa, I'm Elliott." He reached an open hand to Pippa.

"Coach Swift? Oh!" She accepted his hand and shook it with enthusiasm. "I've heard all about you for two days while the team has been getting this place decked out. They speak very highly of you, it's a true pleasure to meet you. And congrats on the championship."

Elliott nodded, his face turning pink.

"Coach?"

A tall, handsome young man that oozed confidence stood about three feet away, with a cocky smirk on his face. While everyone else wore black, he wore a white tux like he didn't give a flying fuck what people thought and the gleam in his eye was almost daring someone to comment.

"Yes, please." Cat's murmur from behind her made Clare cringe.

This boy was going to be trouble.

"Ah. Theo. You're here, good. You got my message?" Elliott stepped to the side and gestured toward Cat. "This is Catriona."

Theo's mouth dropped open like something from a cartoon. She wouldn't be surprised if his eyes did that 'pop out of their sockets, shoot forward, then slam back into his head' thing, too.

Cat fluttered her lashes as she stepped forward and extended her hand. "Cat. It's nice to meet you, Theo."

Theo was clearly in trouble. His face was redder than Cat's dress and a thin sheen of sweat was quickly prickling across his forehead as his mouth opened and closed without sound.

"Theo?"

"Ye-yeah, Coach?" Theo swallowed twice.

Elliott tipped his head toward Cat's still-outstretched hand.

"Oh! Shit. Yeah. Hi." He wiped his palm on his pant leg before shaking Cat's hand. "I'm beautiful." He coughed. "I mean. Fuck. Shit. Sorry."

The apology was thrown Clare's direction. Pippa folded her arms and watched the exchange with a huge smirk and a twinkle in her eye.

"I mean..." A nervous laugh, a glance around the semi-circle at each of the grownups, and another swallow before he tried again. "You're beautiful. I'm Theo." His shoulders heaved like the relief of being able to introduce himself was palpable. "Thanks for coming."

Cat's face twisted with something Clare couldn't place. Was she amused? Disgusted? Did she need to fart? But then Cat nodded, looped her arm through the elbow Theo offered, and they walked toward the door to the ballroom.

"Wow." Pippa exhaled. "That was quite the train wreck."

"Right? When I first saw him I thought he'd be trouble, but now...I'm not so sure." Clare slipped her thumb nail between her teeth.

Pippa bumped hips with Clare. "Oh, he's totally gonna be trouble alright." She winked. "Go ahead inside. I have some more guests arriving."

On their walk through the double doors that led to the ballroom, Elliott's palm made its way to the small of her back, sending a tiny shiver snaking up her spine.

"How do you know Pippa?" he asked.

"Honestly?"

His brows pinched. "Of course."

She stopped and turned to face him. "I came to Pippa's Place when I got pregnant with Cat. I was scared, alone, I didn't know how to tell my parents I got knocked up." She shrugged, fighting the draw of the old memories tugging her back to darker times. "I considered termination. Coming here, talking to Pippa... She saved me."

Blinking back the welling tears she tugged his arm so they'd move again. She couldn't bear looking at the sadness in those hazel depths for another nanosecond.

"Coach, you made it."

Elliott's eye roll rivaled her own daughter's before he schooled his face and turned to the two men who stood close by, but Clare was grateful for the interruption, needing a moment to compose herself.

"Lincoln. Russell." He nodded at each of them but they didn't leave.

The blond one wiggled his eyebrows, and the darker haired one tilted his head at Clare and widened his eyes.

Clare giggled as Elliott's scowl deepened.

"Can I help you boys?"

Elliott had resorted to grinding his words out between gritted teeth, and Clare rolled her lips to stop the brewing laughter from escaping.

"We uh..." The blond's brows rose with expectation before Elliott sighed.

"If I introduce you, will you leave us alone?"

Two heads bobbed with solemn nods. "For now at least."

The corner of Elliott's mouth twitched. "Clare, this is Lincoln Scott and Russell Stewart. Linc, Russ, this is my better half, Clare."

A ripple of warmth passed through her. Better half. She

wouldn't go that far, but it was nice that he basically claimed her as his girlfriend to two of his players. She stepped forward to shake their hands.

"It's nice to meet you. Elliott has told me so much about you both."

Lincoln paused before accepting her hand. "Only believe half of it."

"He speaks very highly of all of his players."

The two men's eyes widened. "I bet that's not true, but thanks for saying it." Russell shook her hand.

"Where did you meet?" Lincoln clearly wasn't going to let it drop without details.

"Lincoln..." A muscle in Elliott's cheek twitched, and she couldn't help but laugh again. Seeing him in his work role tickled her.

Placing a hand on his chest, she gave a little pat. "It's okay, Eli." With a shake of her head she gave the boys a smile. "Elliott and I have known each other since we were little. We fell out of touch for a while but we recently reconnected."

Two blank faces stared at her with what looked like a mixture of awe, confusion, and excitement. "You knew him as a kid?" Linc rubbed his chin.

"You mean...he wasn't born a fully grown adult?" Russ shook his head. "Who knew?"

Rubbing his hands together, Linc turned his head from Eli to Clare and back again. "Does this mean she has dirt on you, Coach? Do we get childhood stories?"

"I like you Linc, I really do. But I'm about three seconds away from giving Theo your C."

Lincoln's jaw hung open and Russ grunted. "Coach. You wouldn't. You couldn't!"

"I will if you don't get the hell out of my space."

From his tone he might have been half joking. Maybe. She

couldn't tell. The boys smiled and nodded at her before turning away.

"Oh, wait. Linc?"

"Yeah, Coach?"

Eli leveled him with a glare and pointed his finger. "Speaking of Theo. Keep an eye on him, please. He's here with Clare's daughter Catriona, and I don't want him doing anything stupid."

"Yes, Coach."

"I mean, she can handle herself, but... It's Theo."

Linc and Russ nodded again like truer words had never been spoken and left them alone. Pippa flitted by with glasses of champagne in hand, pausing to give one to Elliott and Clare before gliding away again. Clare was convinced the woman's feet weren't even on the ground.

"What's Theo's story?" Twinkling lights lit up the room, and she wondered if she could liberate the disco ball for her bedroom before the night was out.

Elliott stiffened beside her, his bicep tensing against hers before he shrugged. "I have no idea. Big chip on his shoulder, lots to prove, cocky as hell." He took a long swig of his champagne. "Kid has more talent in his pinkie than I do in my whole body. He's going to make it big, I just need to make sure one of his teammates doesn't kill him before that happens."

Prom passed in a blur of laughter and dancing. Elliott had treated her like a queen, pulling her chair out, opening doors, refilling her drink, and making sure that his players didn't overwhelm her with questions. It had been worth the butt hurt of asking the sperm donor to take Mason for a weekend that wasn't his.

She'd collected her sandals and clutch in one hand, and looped the other through Elliott's outstretched arm with a yawn. The kids were still dancing, someone—her suspicion was Pippa—had ordered a stack of pizzas, and Lincoln had given her his word that he'd make sure Catriona got home safely.

Even though she was a grown woman, Clare couldn't help but worry about her, damn near every day since she'd been born. Cat had shooed her away with a grin. She was fine, Mom, don't worry, Mom, go have *fun*, Mom.

Fun. Clare gulped. She hadn't had *that* type of fun in a long time. And while she'd shaved her legs and made sure her downstairs...area...was at least tidy and not overrun, with each step they took toward the car, her stomach fluttered.

"Hungry?"

She heaved a breath as she lowered herself into the car. "Famished. That pizza smelled so damn good. We should have taken a box with us. Or at least a slice."

Eli leaned on the car door. The top two buttons of his crisp white shirt were open and his bowtie hung undone around his neck. He had his suit jacket draped over one arm and his shirt sleeves rolled up his forearms. That glimpse of lean, muscular arms made her crazy.

"I was too busy trying to run interference and stop you from stealing Pippa's disco ball to be of sound enough mind to steal pizza from my boys. They'd probably have cut your arm off if you'd tried."

"I don't believe it for a minute." She laughed as he closed the door, tossed his jacket in the back seat and circled the car to get into the driver's side. "They are all very sweet kids."

"They are good kids. But hockey players aren't really sweet." He eased the car out of the parking lot and into the street. "And we don't tell them they're good kids too often, okay? As much as I'd love to be their friend, I can't. I'm their Coach. I gotta be the bad guy, the hard ass, the one who pushes them to be the best they can be." He flicked on the turn signal and slowed to a stop at a red light.

"You're basically a parent to almost thirty teenage boys."

He nodded. "I mean, some are in their twenties too, but yeah. That about covers it."

They rode in charged silence until they got to KFC. A guy stood outside the door, holding a tray of chicken. Her growling stomach had her reaching for a piece and taking a huge bite out of the chicken strip before the man reacted.

"What the fuck, lady?"

She froze and her mouth dropped open. "These aren't samples?"

Elliott was bent over, laughing so hard he couldn't speak.

"Not samples. Dinner." The young guy shook his head.

"Oh, God." The bite of chicken lodged itself in Clare's chest as bands of mortification tightened around her body. She'd just taken some random dude's chicken.

"Who the fuck offers samples at KFC in the middle of the goddamn night?"

Elliott met her eyes and laughed harder. Tears streamed down his face as he clutched his side. "You just ate that guy's dinner," he choked out.

The guy who Clare had deprived of a chicken strip was laughing too.

"I am so sorry." Her voice was barely a whisper. Did she offer the half-eaten chicken strip back to him? Did she eat it right there and hope it pushed the still-lodged first half down the rest of the way to her stomach?

Elliott was no help. The man clearly found this funnier than anything else in his entire life. He wiped his eyes. "I'll get you more chicken, man. I'm sorry. She just has no manners."

Clare slapped Elliott's chest before covering his mouth with her palm. "Don't. Just don't."

Elliott laughed even harder and she couldn't fight a smile.

"I really am so sorry."

The guy waved her off, and she grabbed Elliott by the arm

and dragged him inside. "It's not that funny." She gave him her best mom-face.

"It's absolutely this funny and more. You took another man's chicken, Clare. You're basically married to him now."

She bumped him with her elbow. "I hate you." Her heartrate was returning to normal, and the wave of heat that had engulfed her when she realized that she'd just walked up to a stranger and taken his chicken was starting to cool off.

Did other people do that kind of shit? Or was she the only person things like this happened to?

Eli ordered for both of them, and an extra basket of tenders for the good sport out front. As they waited, he pulled out his phone and his thumbs glided over the screen.

"Texting the other woman?" She knew he wasn't. But standing in the middle of a fast food restaurant dressed for a red carpet event, and—with any luck—on her way to getting laid by the man she'd loved since he was a boy, her insecurities yelled louder.

"Cat, actually."

Her Cat? Her daughter? Why was her...boyfriend? Was that what he was? Why was her boyfriend—she cringed at the word—texting her daughter?

"She has to know about Chicken-Gate." He shrugged like he was simply telling an old friend. Cat had given him her number? Did they talk? Were they friends? She wasn't sure how she felt about it.

He closed the space between them and dropped a kiss on her forehead. "Stop overthinking it. We texted once before this. That's all."

Oh, that was all, was it? Well, that made it totally fine then, didn't it? What was the conversation about? She needed to know. She'd just learned about it and it was already burning her from the inside.

"What did you talk about?" Cool. Subtle. Like a motherfuckin' ninja.

He tapped her on the nose. "Be patient, chicken thief. I need to make sure you're not going to be arrested for stealing first."

She pursed her lips and chuckled. "It's never going away, is it?"

He shook his head. "It'll grow, every time I tell it, too. Pretty soon you'll have wrestled a live chicken from a little old man."

When they left the restaurant, the guy was still there, arms folded, foot braced against the side of the building. Elliott laughed again as he gave the man fresh chicken.

At the car, he handed her their bag of chicken before closing the passenger door and getting back in the driver side.

"Where are we going?" She reached into the bag and pulled out the tenders, *her* tenders.

"Your place. Cat's staying at a friend's. That's what we were texting about. She wanted to give us privacy." He smiled, but his tone was hesitant.

"Oh." Suddenly she was a scared teenager all over again. Did he not want things to progress between them? Did he not want to get her naked?

JFC if he didn't give her an orgasm after being a walking tease all freakin' night, she was going to lose her fucking mind.

"I got you something."

"Other than my corsage?"

"Reach behind my seat."

Groping in the dark with a bag of hot chicken on her lap wasn't easy, but she produced the box from the floor after some grunting and stretching. "What is it?"

"People tend to open their gifts to discover what's inside, Ceecee."

The long rectangular box housed a pickle shaped vibrator.

A five inch long, green, nubby personal massager. She burst out laughing.

"You bought me a sex toy?"

"I didn't see this one on your bed. The reviews aren't stellar, but I figured considering your collection you needed to add a vibrating pickle to the drawer."

She clutched the toy to her chest as she laughed. "I can't believe you got me a pickle pecker."

"I did. But you won't need it."

CHAPTER 11
Clare

Clare plucked at invisible lint on her thigh as they sat in the car in the driveway of her home. It wasn't that she didn't *want* to sleep with Elliott —though it had been so long since she'd gotten laid that he'd probably need to dust off the cobwebs from her hoo-ha. Could your hymen grow back? Was she a born again virgin?

Giving him her body wasn't what she was afraid of. She was afraid of giving him her heart and having him crush it all over again.

He cleared his throat. "You don't have to... I mean..." He rubbed the back of his neck. "We don't have to..."

Her face heated. "I know. It's not... I want to."

"What is it, CeeCee?"

Knuckles skimmed under her chin as he caught her before she could turn away from him. "Talk to me."

Her lip trembled as she struggled to compose herself. "I'm scared, Elliott."

He stayed quiet, the warm glow of the streetlight lighting up his face, pinched with concern. After a beat, he nodded. "We haven't really talked about anything, have we?"

She shook her head, dislodging tears down her cheeks that she'd fought so hard to keep under wraps. She got it, she didn't want to open the door to all of their gut-wrenching past any more than he did. But it hung over them, over *her*, like a dark cloud.

"Y-you left me." Her voice was barely a whisper. "I'm scared you're going to leave me again." She lowered her gaze to her lap. "Everyone leaves me eventually."

Even Mason.

She'd always been the stern mom, the disciplinarian, the *eat your vegetables and clean your room* mom. And Alex, well, he had been the fun parent. It only made sense that Mason would choose to live where he could have sugar crusted cereal every day for breakfast, and no set bed time. That didn't mean it didn't hurt. Or that it didn't compound a lifetime of being abandoned by the men in her life.

"I was a dumb kid, Clare. I shouldn't have just taken off. Especially not without talking to you." He cupped her face with his hand. "I was a coward. I didn't want to fight with you. I wanted to go and make... *something* of myself."

She almost laughed. "But you were *everything* to me."

"I'm so sorry." His words were strangled, dripping with the same tortured agony she felt deep in her chest. "I wanted to play hockey, and I knew you didn't want me to leave. I was selfish and short sighted." He swallowed, his Adam's apple bobbing in the dim light as a battle played out across his features. "We're adults now, though, Clare. It's different. I learned from my mistakes and I would never do something like that again."

She hadn't thought he'd ever do something like that the first time. But everything inside her wanted to believe that he'd changed, that this time he'd stay, that this time he'd choose her.

"You really hurt me, Eli."

He nodded. "I know. And I can't go back and change anything I put you through. But I can try to be better, to *do* better."

After a long silence, she sighed. "I always dreamed we'd build a life together you know. Have a family, live close to our parents, a dog... hell, even the white picket fence."

"There's still time to have a family together, CeeCee."

His confidence wrapped around her like a warm blanket, but it was misplaced. Wasn't it?

How was there still time to have the things she'd dreamed of as a young girl? She was getting old enough that even if she had wanted more children, doctors would caution her against it. She would be a *geriatric* pregnancy.

Did she want more kids?

Did she want to be a *geriatric* mother?

Did she want to start all over again? With achy boobs, explosive diapers, and no sleep?

It wasn't something she'd given thought to for a long time. Not having reliable father figures in her kid's lives didn't make for great *happily ever after* fantasy fodder.

He'd given her so much to think about, but she didn't want to think any more about it tonight. Not now. Not when she looked a million fucking dollars, had waxed to within an inch of newborn skin, had a free house, and Elliott looked delicious enough to eat.

Another long pause hung between them before she shifted in her seat and reached for the door handle. "Do you want to come inside?"

CHAPTER 12
Elliott

The gold dress had gone from taunting him all night long, hugging her every curve, to being a crumpled pile at his feet. Lying in the middle of the bed in her underwear, Clare made his mouth water. Intricate scraps of nude lace material covered her breasts and crotch as she lay on the bed in front of him.

"You're staring." She curled her hand over her stomach.

"Damn fucking straight I'm staring. You're a fucking goddess lying there, Clare." He couldn't help but lick his lips. He itched to spread her legs and feast on her pussy.

Her cheeks pinked. "You're also very naked."

He chuckled. "Isn't that kinda the point?"

She bit her lip and nodded.

"Unless you're changing your mind?" His stomach sank. Was she changing her mind? Cold feet? Regret? Had she not actually found it in her heart to forgive him for chasing his dreams all those years ago?

A small head shake was all she gave up. Her eyes devoured every contour of his body, and paused on his dick. He wasn't hung like a horse by any means, but he knew what to do with it. "I'm gonna rip those panties off you and eat you like the delicacy you are. Then I'm gonna fuck you senseless until your legs don't work."

Her flush darkened, but her eyebrow rose as though challenging him. He leaned forward, curled his fingers around the flimsy material and tugged. The fabric didn't give, but Clare shrieked.

"Ow! What the hell? Books and movies don't tell you about friction burn in your ass crack when someone tries to rip off your pretty undies." She wiggled on the bed. "It's always so fucking hot in books. The fabric just gives way and it's easy. That did not feel easy." She sniffed.

"Take two?"

She shook her head and looped her thumbs through the elastic.

The hell he was letting her take them off herself. "Don't. Leave them. I'll do it."

Her hands fell by her sides, and he picked up her foot, dotting kisses along the inside length of her leg enjoying the shiver that rippled through her body at his touch. When he got to her inner thigh, he traced her name along her skin with his tongue, her whimpers and tiny breaths making him painfully hard.

Slipping his fingers between her panties and her pussy, he paused to inhale. He'd wanted to touch her, to worship her, to make her come for so damn long that he could commit every single detail to memory. She reached for him like she needed him, kissing his skin with her gentle touch.

As pretty as her underwear was, he made light work of them, tossing her panties and bra to the floor on top of her dress and settled between her thighs. Spreading her lips with one hand, he blew on her clit. Goosebumps spread across her stomach and she arched her spine, angling her pelvis so her pussy was closer to his face.

Instead of relenting to her need, he blew on her again. With his free hand he skimmed the pad of his finger on her clit, dragging it through her arousal, enjoying her groan when he circled her opening but didn't slip inside her. Her muscles twitched.

"Elliott, p-p-please." She reached again, but when he bent his head away from her, her fist met the bed with a frustrated puff of air.

He drew his tongue through her folds, savoring her sweet arousal and lapped once at her clit. A long, slow stroke with his flat tongue. Her body jolted as she arched her hips and gripped his hair.

"Shhhhhh. Patience. I want to take my time and enjoy you, Ceecee. We aren't in a hurry, just enjoy it." He licked her again, walking his fingers up the sides of her soft, smooth body, skimming over her plush middle, the bumps of her ribs, and across her chest until he found her already hard nipples.

Quickly finding a rhythm, he ate her delicious pussy and nipped, tugged, and caressed her plump tits with his thumbs and forefingers at the same time. Her slow and even breaths turned into ragged, sharp intakes of breath as her body quivered and jerked under him.

"I'm close."

He hummed against her soaking pussy and pulled back his right hand from her nipple. "Are you ready for my fist, Clare?"

A shudder rippled through her. "Fuck, yes."

She balled her hands in the sheet at her sides as he sank his fingers into her. Three at first, but quickly added the fourth, and when she moaned, he tucked his thumb, pushing against the pressure from her walls and curled his hand into a fist inside her.

His dick was rock hard against the soft sheets, if he moved even a little, he'd probably get enough friction to blow his load. As he pushed his fist further inside her, her muscles tightened and she lifted her hips from the bed. He might never get his hand back. He tried to ease it back and forth but her pussy had his arm in a goddamn death grip.

"More." Her plea was accompanied by her nails scratching on the bed by her sides, he'd make sure they dragged across his skin before the end of the night. "Please Eli. Harder."

He pumped his fist inside her in slow, measured strokes, pausing to savor her contracting muscles gripping his forearm. But the more her hips bucked to meet him, the faster his movements grew. He flicked her nipple with his hand and her clit with his tongue before opening his fist and pushing his fingers against her g-spot.

She stilled for a fraction of a second, but then her legs gripped his head with a force that might be concerning if he wasn't so focused on making her come undone on his tongue.

He grinned as her body jerked and tremored. Her hands clutched at his hair with such an urgency that even if she did cut off the oxygen to his body with her thighs, he'd find a way to stay alive long enough to keep going until she came.

It was his only goal left in life. To taste her cum on his face as she screamed his name, and he'd stop at nothing to accomplish it. Nothing else mattered.

Her entire body tensed as her moans escalated to a chorus of "yes" and his name, over and over, like she was chanting him across the finish line. She came on a wail as her nails dug into his scalp, and her legs pinned him against her pussy with such strength he was almost worried he'd get stuck there.

If there was a better place to get stuck, he hadn't found it.

As her body softened, he slid his hand from her and dropped kisses up her thighs, over her hip bones, taking a moment to pause over her C-section scar and dot a line of kisses along it. "I know it's easier said than done." He kissed his way back over the scar. "But you need to be kinder to your body. It's been through a lot. It's made actual people, Ceecee. You should treasure it."

Trailing his tongue up the side of her belly button, he smiled as her body sagged deeper into the mattress, and her eyes fluttered shut. His painfully hard dick pressed against her thigh as he moved along her body, enjoying the fine sheen of sweat coating her skin. He dragged his tongue across her collarbone and up the curve of her neck, a vibration passed through her, and he repeated the movement.

He nipped at her earlobe before working his way around her jaw and finally capturing her mouth with his. Her fingers sank into his shoulders, pulling him against her, and between deep and passionate kisses she told him she was on birth control.

Her body shook with laughter and their foreheads knocked together as she giggled.

Pulling back he searched her face. "What? I can't say I've ever been laughed at in bed before."

"I told you I was on birth control. But it didn't make a damn bit of difference when I got pregnant."

He chuckled and brushed his nose against hers. "And here I was thinking you were laughing at my manhood."

She kissed him, and her warmth spread throughout his chest and into his limbs like the sun peeking out from behind a cloud. "There's absolutely nothing laughable about what's pressed up against my thigh, Eli. Though if you don't get inside me soon, we're going to have a problem."

Hooking his hands behind her knees he shifted her weight down the bed and spread her legs apart. His pulsing cock rested between her lips, ready, aching, straining to slide inside her.

Cupping his face in her hands, she frowned. "What is it?"

He shook his head. "I've wanted this for such a long time, Clare. I just want to appreciate every second."

She nodded and closed her glistening eyes. "Me too."

He kissed her, deep and slow, like two decades of pain and history weren't hanging over them. He kissed her as though he'd never left to play hockey, as though she'd been his girl for their whole lives and no one else had kissed her.

He kissed her the way he should have twenty years earlier—and the way he intended to kiss her for the rest of his life.

"Good morning." He bent over and kissed her temple as she sat cross-legged on a dining room chair in an oversized sweater. The mug of coffee she cradled was so big it could easily be mistaken for a bucket.

She sucked in a yawn and scratched her head through her messy bun before answering. "Good morning. Coffee's in the pot."

"You sure there's enough left for me?" He jerked his chin at her cup while he picked up the second mug from the counter.

"Don't judge the size of my coffee mug, Elliott."

"No judgment, just amusement. That mug is big enough to go for a swim in."

Her sleepy smile brightened the kitchen. She hadn't been wrong about her house. The place definitely needed a little TLC and fixing up. A leak in the faucet, boxes of tiles stacked in the corner—presumably to replace her floor—faded paint on the walls, and a few other small things that needed to be fixed.

Something dropping on the floor upstairs made him jump. "The fuck? Did Cat come home early? She said she wouldn't be back this early. Should I leave?" While he'd thrown on a t-shirt before coming downstairs, he was still in his boxers and didn't want to be busted by Cat in his undies.

Clare waved him off and he sat in the chair facing her. "That's just Lola. My cleaner." She snorted.

He cocked his head. "What's so funny?"

"This place needs more than a cleaner coming in once a month for a few hours to sort it out. It's a mess. I keep saying I'm going to just take a room at a time and fix it up, but I never get around to it. I'm amazed that Lola ever manages to actually get to the dirt."

Elliott would love to get a housekeeper into his parent's house, but Dad would never stand for a stranger being in his space. "What kinds of things does she do for you?"

He sipped on the elixir of life, breathing the steam deep into his lungs. Was there a better smell on earth than freshly made coffee?

"Mostly the bathrooms. My kids are animals. Lazy animals. But if she has extra time she'll dust the rest of the space, empty or load the dishwasher if there are dishes around. She's overworked and under paid. Just like the rest of us." She closed her eyes and took a drink. "Someday I'll get this place fixed up and it'll always be drop-in ready. But that day is not today."

The heaviness in her voice twisted something in his stomach. She wasn't complaining about her life, but at the same time he couldn't help but feel for her. She had gone through so much by herself, was so many things to so many people, and yet she never felt enough. It had to be an exhausting way to live.

"Clare? Do you want me to put your vibrators back on charge? I saw the cables hanging out of the drawer." Lola poked her head around the door, her eyes locked onto him and widened. "Oh, God. I'm so sorry. I didn't know you had a visitor."

He offered her a warm smile—with any luck, she wouldn't

feel too uncomfortable. He was the one, after all, sitting in his underwear.

"It's okay, Lola." Clare laughed but her face was bright red. "Yes, please. There's a new one next to the gold clutch on the dresser. It needs to be charged as well."

Lola rolled her eyes and tutted. "There are only so many cables, Clare. I'll have to do them in batches." The older lady shook her head and left.

"Thanks, Lola!" Clare grinned. "She's the best."

"She sure seems like it. I mean, there's nothing worse than going to get yourself off and your toys are all dead, right?"

"See?" She raised her mug to him. "You get it."

He nodded solemnly. "Only too well."

She burst out laughing. Leaning forward, she gave him a push. "I'm feeling judgment from you, Elliott Swift. You don't get to judge my vibrators any more than you get to judge the amount of coffee I drink. Especially not when you buy me a new vibrator to add to my collection."

Holding up his hands, he shook his head. "I'm impressed and low-key intimidated by your toy collection, Clare Reynolds. But there is absolutely no judgment from me. I just wish you didn't need them."

Her piercing blue eyes met his over their mugs and unspoken words hung between them, stifling him. Her eyes said "well maybe if you hadn't left, I wouldn't need to fuck myself with silicone." He cringed. They probably didn't say that, but his guilt raged in his stomach and it was what he felt.

It was true. If he'd stayed, he'd have been with her, and her need to self-service wouldn't have even been a thing.

"I'm looking forward to using some of them on you." He put down his mug and guided her hands to do the same before tugging her hand and bringing her around the table to him. He eased her onto his lap, straddling him, her bare legs dangling on either side of his as his hardening dick nestled at the apex of her thighs.

Strands from her messy top knot fell loosely around her face as she dipped her head to kiss him. Looping her arms around his neck, she shifted her weight, pressing her hips against his as she leaned into the kiss.

His fingertips skimmed along the length of her legs, before he cupped her hips and pulled her against him. She moved her pelvis, grinding against his erection, eliciting a moan from him between kisses, and he slid his hands to her ass, squeezing her cheeks as she moved.

"Clare…what…about…Lola…?"

She didn't stop. In fact she rode harder. The damp heat through her panties against his crotch drove him wild. He needed to be inside her. Bracing her against him, he stood, and she shrieked, gripping him tighter.

He placed her on the kitchen counter, tugging her by her ankles until her ass met the ledge. It wasn't the perfect height for him to fuck her, but they could make it work. He reached into his boxers and freed his cock, pumping it twice without taking his eyes off hers.

"Look at what you do to me, Ceecee."

When her eyes didn't stray from his face, he repeated himself. "Look, Clare." A droplet of precum squeezed out his slit as he pumped his dick again.

Lust clouded her eyes as she nibbled on her bottom lip.

"Are you wet for me?"

"You know I am." Her breathless answer, her heaving chest, her pinking skin, her spread legs and her wandering fingers towards her pink panties… He couldn't wait another second to be inside her.

Lola be damned. He didn't care if she got a bird's eye view of his bare ass as he fucked Clare on the kitchen counter.

The front door slammed. "Mom, we're home!"

That he cared about.

"Shit!" Clare slid off the counter, bonking her head against his as she dismounted, narrowly missing his stiff-as-a-rod hard on. That wouldn't have been fun for him.

Face pale, eyes wide, she shrugged.

"I'll go get dressed," he told her. "Be right back. Try not to panic."

She nodded.

"Want me to climb out your bedroom window and shimmy down the drainpipe?"

"Mom? Is that Elliott's car outside?" Cat's singsong voice echoed around the kitchen.

Too late, he was busted. Climbing out the window wouldn't make a damn bit of difference at this point.

"I'm going to put pants on." He pecked her forehead and bolted for the stairs taking them two at a time. He pulled a pair of jeans from his overnight bag before collecting the scattered remnants of his tux and cramming them in his bag.

His hair stood up at all angles, but at least he was clothed and his protesting dick was behind denim bars.

Was this what it was like to have kids? Cock blocking little shits. Next time he'd make sure to carry Clare to a room that had a lock on the door so their arrival back home wouldn't matter.

He was pretty sure he could get them both off quickly enough if the need arose. He just needed to be more aware of the possibility for disruption. He felt bad for getting Clare worked up and leaving her hanging.

Maybe he'd call her later tonight and they'd get off on the phone again. Or maybe he'd sneak over after dark and fuck her against the side of her house. Or maybe—

"Eli, you want pancakes?" Clare's voice carried up the stairs.

Did bears shit in the woods? Pancakes were his love language. "Please!"

As he stepped out into the hallway, he tugged the bedroom door closed behind him. Mason stood at the top of the stairs, arms folded, grin firmly on his face. "You're dating my mom." His whisper carried hope and excitement. For some reason Elliott had expected anger and resentment.

Had she told him they were dating? If he confirmed it, would she fillet his kidneys and feed them to the neighbourhood cats? Fuck. Why hadn't he paused for just a fucking minute to check their story before bolting upstairs to cover his goddamn junk?

"What did your mom tell you?"

He shrugged. "Just that you're seeing where things go."

Things were going. Things were definitely going. But he didn't need to see where things were going to go, he knew. Deep in the pit of his stomach, and in every inch of his heart, body, and soul, he knew. She was his endgame. He was never letting her go again, and he regretted ever having done it before.

The kid's face turned somber.

"What is it, Mason?"

"She's been through a lot." He gnawed on his thumb.

That was easy to agree with, she really had. He nodded, his chest warming at the boy's concern for his mom.

"I know grown-ups can't really plan the future. But can you try not to hurt her? Please? I hate it when she's sad."

This kid.

Elliott stepped toward him and gave what he'd hoped was a reassuring pat on his shoulder. "I'm hoping to help you take care of her if that's okay."

Mason smiled and nodded.

"I'm sure sometimes it's hard for you to do by yourself."

Another nod.

"You do a great job looking after her, Mason." Another shoulder pat.

What else could he say?

"It'll be harder for me to take care of her from my dad's house. So I could definitely use the backup."

His dad's house? That didn't sound good, but the sadness in Mason's eyes, and the fact that it was none of Elliott's goddamned business – even though curiosity burned him from the inside out made him keep his questions to himself. "I got you, kid."

When they descended the stairs Clare was shaking her ass to Destiny's Child in the kitchen. She had put sweat pants on, probably from the laundry room, her sweater had been replaced by a green t-shirt, and she wore a bright red apron as she whisked pancake batter in a huge mixing bowl.

She looked no less a goddess than she had in the slinky, shimmering gold dress and heels the night before. He was a goner for the woman.

Catriona leaned against the counter, singing into a wooden spoon. "Morning, Coach."

He saluted her. "Catriona." He poured his cold coffee into the sink and got a refill. "How was prom?"

She shrugged, but a smile teased her lips. "Fine."

"Theo was a gentleman?" He narrowed his eyes to slits. Theo had better have been a fucking gentleman or Elliott would string him up by his ankles and have the team beat him with hockey sticks.

Oh. That was a damned good idea. He'd most definitely tuck that threat away for the future.

She nodded. "Once he figured out how to use the English language again, anyway."

Clare barked out a laugh. "Poor kid was kinda scared of you at first, wasn't he, Cat?"

"He couldn't complete a sentence for what felt like an

hour. He just kept...staring. So weird." She cringed. "Some of the other players kept stopping by to make sure I was okay." She pinned Elliott with a glare. "Did you have something to do with that?"

He shrugged in answer. "Theo's new to town, to the team. I just didn't want anything to go wrong."

Cat gave a knowing grin and pressed a button on her phone. Paramore's *I'm into You* blasted from the speakers, he'd heard it enough times at the rink to almost know it by heart. Clare covered her face with her palm. He was sure if he could hear her, he'd have heard a groan, too.

She took Cat's phone and pressed the volume button on the side. "Subtle. I think he's well aware I'm still into him, Catriona."

"Just making sure. Call me when it's ready!" She skipped toward the door, but he touched her elbow as she passed.

"For the record, I'm still into your mom, too." He winked at her. Or at least he would have been if she and Mason hadn't interrupted them.

She rolled her eyes. "So. Gross."

"You bring this on yourself, Catriona. Get out of here before we start talking sordid details."

"Don't need 'em. I know exactly what was going on in here before I opened that door. Coach Swift disappeared up those stairs like his butt was on fire."

Clare pointed the whisk at her daughter. "Leave. Or I'll get the baby pictures out and show Eli just how adorable you used to be before this...monster thing...took over your body."

"You love me." She stepped back to kiss Clare on the cheek.

"I want my baby back!"

Cat laughed and left the room. "I'll always be your baby, Mom."

It was as though her announcement was a declaration of

war. Mason's voice bellowed from the living room where—Elliott assumed—he was glued to a screen playing a game. "I'll always be her baby. You'll always be older, Sissy."

"Yes, yes, but I love you both equally." It was Clare's turn to roll her eyes. "Please let it drop. Please let it drop." She chanted but cocked her head, nodding when both kids stayed quiet. "So, that went better than I expected."

"What did?"

"Mason. I thought he'd take..." She waved a finger between them. "This hard, I guess."

He nodded. "I guess we're officially dating."

"I guess we are."

CHAPTER 13
Clare

If she could have bottled the moment and kept it on a shelf forever, she would have. Her head rested on Elliott's bare stomach as she lay draped across him on her bed. Her hair splayed over his damp-with-sweat skin from another round of being treasured like a queen.

Her thighs ached, her lady bits ached, and she probably needed to guzzle a gallon of water to rehydrate, but as he traced his fingers back and forth over her chest, she'd never felt more relaxed and at ease.

She sighed, sinking into him just that little bit more.

"I need to tell you something."

The six words every woman loves to hear made her hot and sticky body turn cold and tense. Swallowing hard, she nodded. "Okay?"

She tried to sit up, but he held her in place against him, his palm on her sternum.

"I don't know that I can tell you if you're looking at me. Please just stay there?"

"'Kay." Fuck. Shit. Panic. Was he leaving again? Was he

taking his super talented tongue, and devilishly handsome smile and going to use it to make someone else's clit go crazy?

She wouldn't let him. Not again. This was her line in the sand. He had to get her off him before he could leave and she was very good at making herself into a dead weight. He had no chance.

A hysterical laugh squeaked from her.

"What?"

"I was just thinking that if you tried to leave I'd just keep lying on you so you couldn't."

"A fool proof plan, I grant you, but totally unnecessary. I'm not leaving."

"Then what do you need to tell me?"

He went quiet for a moment, sighed, and slid his fingers through her hair, rubbing at her scalp.

She moaned. "No. I'm not letting you distract me from whatever bomb you're about to drop on my head by massaging it with your magic fingers first."

"You think my fingers are magic?" Amusement laced his words, but she was too anxious to find the funny in the moment. What could he want to tell her?

"Focus, Elliott. I'm getting worked up. And not in the fun way."

He shushed her and went back to stroking her hair. "Don't panic, I promise I'm not leaving."

"Then what is it?" Her voice was small, childish, fragile. She hated how his leaving her had impacted her self-worth so severely all those years ago, but she hadn't found a way to let go of it, even as a fully grown adult.

"I came back." He cleared his throat. "Back... then... in high school." His voice was slow, heavy, thick with emotion, and charged with caution.

He'd come back? What did that mean? Of course he'd come back. If memory served, Catriona was still a drooling, shitting, sleep-hating monster at the time. Clare had seen Eli in the store over Thanksgiving break when she was in college.

Is that what he meant? He'd come back for vacation? He didn't go to college locally so he didn't mean that. And if he hadn't come back home they wouldn't have been having this conversation.

"Twice, in fact."

She barely breathed, letting him continue, though her heart pounded so fast she wasn't sure she'd survive long enough to hear the end of his explanation.

"I went to your work to see you. The shop was busy, but I still saw you behind the counter. Flushed cheeks, bright smile, and so very heavily pregnant I wondered how you were defying gravity."

The words sat for a moment before the realization dawned. He'd come back, and left again? When she was pregnant with Cat? When she was alone and afraid? Isolated and ostracised—both for becoming pregnant in the first place, and for deciding to have the baby.

He'd come back?

"You... But..." She bolted upright, folding her arms as though that would somehow protect her naked vulnerability. "But you never said hi. You never told me you were back. You just... You left again, for college?" Her voice climbed higher, louder with every word.

His ashen face was crinkled by a frown, and his lips pursed together. To his credit, he didn't break eye contact with her. He sat up in bed and swept a soft hand across her cheek. "I thought you were in a happy relationship and I didn't want to wedge myself into that."

Bitterness rose up in her throat. A happy relationship.

Happy?

Cat's dad had bolted like he was being pursued in a high speed car chase. And never came fucking back.

"H-happy?"

"I'm sorry. I walked in that day, saw you pregnant with some other guy's child, and I lost it. I thought you were happy with him, together. I thought you'd made your choice and picked someone else. I was just a kid too, Ceecee, but I didn't want to fuck things up for you all over again."

Tears poured down her cheeks. "I was so alone."

He nodded and pulled her to his chest. She let him. His arms banded around her, holding her as she sobbed.

"I think my parents kept the truth from me. They knew your parents, right? They knew you weren't happy. They knew you were struggling and alone but they didn't tell me. I think it was because they knew I'd stay if they did."

"S-so you just left again?"

He nodded. "Kind of. I didn't know any different, and I had been given another offer. Turned it down to come back home, but when I saw you, I didn't think there was anything left for me here. And staying here while you were..." He swallowed, the agony in his voice mirrored what she carried in her chest. "With someone else. Having everything we talked about having as kids... I just couldn't face it. So I ran."

"And then?" A whirlwind of emotions careened through her like a tornado. He'd come back. He'd come back, seen she was super pregnant, and left without even talking to her about it.

Fuck.

"When I came back from college, you were married. Mom told me it wasn't to Catriona's father, but she said you were happy, and I'm not a homewrecker." Sourness coated his voice. They had both married homewreckers.

"I had no idea you weren't happy, Clare. None. I mean, I'm not sure what I could have done. I wasn't even sure if you loved me back, but I should have tried. I should have stood in front of you and told you I was back. If nothing else I should have been your best friend and not left you alone during the hardest time of your life. I'm so sorry."

Tears trickled down his beautiful face. He'd carried this with him for as long as she'd carried her betrayal and abandonment when he never came back. The weight of regret and guilt was a heavy load to bear.

Wait. He loved her?

Her head snapped up to his, his hazel eyes dark and still watery. "You l-loved me?"

He grunted, his shoulders sagged and his body deflated. "Only since the day you kicked my shin in grade school."

He loved her.

He came back.

But he'd also left again. He'd seen her at work, carrying Cat, and instead of talking to her about it, he'd fled. Could she hold it against him? What would she have done? What would any other teenage boy have done?

Considering Catriona's father fled the minute she told him she was pregnant, she shouldn't be too surprised that Eli freaked out, too.

He loved her. Did he still love her?

No matter which way her brain churned through everything he'd said, that was the thing she kept coming back to. He'd said it so matter of fact, so sure, so easy. Even though he'd left her when she'd needed him, it was because he'd believed she was happy, because he was putting her happiness with her husband first.

If her heart swelled any bigger, her chest would burst.

His eyes flicked back and forth between hers, like he was looking for something, anything to tell him where she was at, but couldn't find it.

He loved her enough to leave her.

What the hell did she do with that?

"I don't know what you're thinking." His voice cracked as he spoke.

Tears still trickled down her face. She sniffed, wiping her nose with the heel of her hand. "Honestly? I'm thinking that I've been hopping from bad relationship to bad relationship, and maybe the right person for me was the one I kicked when I was little. That's so fucking tragic."

Shuddering sobs raked through her body as he held her again.

"I'm so sorry, Clare. If I could go back, I'd be there for you. I'd... I dunno, rub your swollen feet, and feed you ice cream or whatever you do with pregnant women."

She giggled against his shoulder.

"I can't change the past, we both know that. And you have two beautiful, smart, funny, and kind kids from the journey you took. But I really would like to be a part of your future if you'll let me. Because no matter how far away I ran, I couldn't outrun the fact that I love you."

He pulled her back from his shoulder and gave her a watery smile. "Always have. Always will."

Her stomach fluttered. He still loved her.

"Now?"

He nodded. "Now. Tomorrow. Always." Cupping her face, he guided her lips to his, and kissed her so tenderly it hurt her very soul. Sure, they couldn't change the past, and considering everything she'd gotten from it, she wouldn't, even if she could. But they could build a future, together, at last.

Her stomach flipped. Not everyone got a second chance with their childhood sweetheart. As he kissed her, she slid her arms tighter around his neck and vowed to herself that she wouldn't let either of them fuck it up again.

❄

"This is so freakin' cool!" Mason bounded up into the carriage with an energy Clare wished she possessed.

"Language, Mason."

"I only said freakin', Mom. Not the F-word you always use."

Okay, so her sassy kid wasn't wrong. She did have a mild obsession with the word fuck.

"A horse-drawn carriage ride. Nice." Catriona let Elliott help her up into the wagon before Clare pulled herself up behind her.

Just as she heaved herself into the air, Eli grabbed her ass and made her squeal.

Mason guffawed while Cat muttered "gross." She seemed to flip-flop on whether she wanted Clare to be dating or not. She went from encouraging Clare to "have fun," hell, she even gave Elliott her number at the pharmacy, but now they were together it was suddenly gross. Clare hoped she was joking, but made a mental note to check in with her daughter about whether or not she really was okay with Clare dating Elliott.

Cat turned her attention back to her phone. She was spending way too much time glued to that thing lately. Clare suspected there was a boy involved, but she was trying not to pry.

Cat would tell her when she was ready. But that didn't stop the burning curiosity. Did she have a boyfriend? Who was he? And how had he survived Cat's caustic wit long enough to get past her prickly defenses? So many questions.

"Everyone ready?" Their guide handed out lap robes to guard against the chill.

Marble, their horse, whinnied like he was impatient to hit the road. He knew his role and he couldn't wait to fulfill it. As they pulled away from the Nicollet Island Inn for their hour-long tour, Clare couldn't help but grin. She was excited like a kid at Christmas over marking #30 off their joint bucket list after so long and could barely keep still in her seat.

Their guide, Eric, was very informative on the history of the area and had a great sense of humor as he told them about their city. He managed to somehow educate them without it feeling anything at all like a history lesson.

The views of the Mississippi River and Minneapolis skyline were stunning. She didn't remember the last time she'd simply existed and took in the world around her. Musicians were scattered along their tour route, and their songs carried on the breeze. She'd lived there for many years and seen many things, but on their journey, she saw things she'd overlooked because she'd always been too busy running from A to B.

Eric clearly enjoyed his work, and as they drove through the streets, people stopped to wave and say hi.

The hour passed in the blink of an eye, and before she knew it they were having a delicious family meal back at the Inn. Family meal. That's what it felt like. It had been a couple weeks since Elliott had told her about coming back during high school, and in that time things felt different somehow, more.

It was as though airing out their history had brought them even closer together. Things were easier between them, and every time he smiled at her she felt it all the way to her toes.

When they'd finished their food, Eli suggested they head out to Izzy's ice cream parlor for dessert. "Izzy's was once rated the best ice cream shop in the US."

"The whole country?" Mason's eyes were wide, and despite the fact he'd eaten a huge dinner, she was sure she could see the anticipatory drool trickling already down his chin. "It's that good?"

Eli ruffled Mason's hair, something he'd become fond of

doing. "The. Whole. Country." He nodded. "Over a hundred flavors to choose from."

Mason's jaw dropped. "Shut the front door."

"And they give samples." Eli shrugged. "But if you're too full..."

"No!" Mason grabbed Elliott's arm. "My dessert belly is totally empty. Can we go? Please? I love ice cream."

"You do?" He winked at Clare. "I had no idea. I thought you hated it."

Mase shoved Eli with a grin, but turned to Clare. "Can we, Mom? Puh-leeeeeeease?"

She giggled at how much Mason had taken to Elliott in a relatively short time. It helped that he coached hockey, he was basically hanging out with his hero on the regular. They'd even played NHL on Mason's games console for a couple hours. Elliott could do no wrong.

Mase had even stopped talking about moving to his father's house, but it was still at the forefront of her mind that he was even considering the shift. With Cat basically living elsewhere already, losing Mason at home would crack her heart wide open.

She nodded. "Of course. But you're not going to try all one hundred flavors in one sitting, Mase-Mallow. You'll make yourself sick."

Elliott nudged Mason as they walked toward the car. "But what a way to go, eh?" They laughed like they'd been best friends their whole lives, and Clare couldn't help but wonder how Elliott had settled with a woman who didn't want kids.

He was so good with younger kids, and, as it turned out from watching him with his players, older kids as well. He had so much love to give, it hurt her insides that he'd been forced to smush it all down and keep it to himself for so long.

She rubbed her tummy as Elliott opened the car door for her.

"You okay?"

"Hm? Oh. Yeah. I'm good, thanks." She slipped into the seat.

His raised eyebrow suggested he didn't believe it for a goddamn second. She tried to reassure him with a smile.

"Got gas? I mean, I have gas too. That was quite the meal." He stood upright and patted his stomach.

"No! I don't have *gas*. I mean, I probably will, considering the amount of food I just ate like I'd never before eaten a meal. But no. I'm just...thinking."

"Well your thinking face looks just like your farting face. Just saying." He shrugged and stepped back to close the door with a grin. Her phone chimed with a notification as Eli pulled the car away from the curb.

We regret to inform you...

She didn't get the job. And while part of her was disappointed that she'd finally taken the leap, put herself out there, and landed flat on her face, she was mostly relieved. She'd have been the best candidate for the job, she knew that much, but it wasn't the best time in her life to step up to more responsibilities. Maybe she'd try again when Mason went to college.

"What's up?"

"Didn't get the promotion." She turned the phone screen toward him.

"You don't seem too upset about it."

She shook her head. "I don't think I am. I mean, I'm anxious about who the new manager is going to be. I live in eternal hope it's not another idiot asshole who needs his hand held through every goddamn thing. But I don't think it's the right time yet, you know?"

His warm smile gave her the affirmation she didn't know she needed, and something relaxed in her chest. "You're right. You're busy enough as it is right now. Any more work, or demands on your time and I think you'd struggle."

She absorbed his words. He wasn't wrong.

"You'd make it work, you always do. But that doesn't mean you should."

Clare rolled her eyes at how well he knew her. She'd definitely have pushed herself to her limits if she'd been offered, and taken, the job. It was a mercy that they hadn't chosen her—she'd have felt obligated to accept it.

He picked up her hand and put it on his thigh, giving her a squeeze. "You are exactly where you're supposed to be."

Her heart melted at his support. Did she want more from her career? Definitely. But the more she sat and took stock of her life, the surer she was that it just wasn't the time.

"What about you? Any progress with...?" She wouldn't say Denise's name out loud—not least of all because the kids were in the back seat and she didn't want to subject Eli to any uncomfortable questions.

"Lawyer is sorting it all out. I'm not sure how it's all going to go other than cost a fucking fortune to resolve." Elliott needed out of his dingy apartment and to clear his snowballing debts. The guy was drowning under a mountain of red bills thanks to his stupidly big heart and she couldn't wave a magic wand to fix it.

Working in medical billing she knew how quickly things could escalate when it came to financial matters and while she wished she could help him, she wasn't exactly rolling in it herself.

After some of the most delicious ice cream she'd ever had on her tongue, Elliott dropped them off at home. She was exhausted. Mason had passed out in the backseat, his head on Catriona's shoulder as she frantically pounded her phone screen, but her eyes were heavy, too. What a great day.

Elliott didn't want to stay—well, he did, but he had an early morning the next day, and when he stayed they didn't do so hot at the sleeping thing. But she texted him goodnight before rolling over to go to sleep. In reply, he'd forwarded her tickets for their next date. A trip out to a cooking class that his dad had bought them to—and he was quoting—get Elliott the fuck out from under his feet.

Eli said he hadn't been over there all that much, but it seemed enough for his dad to want to keep him distracted. For a while at least.

Right as she was dozing off, her cell phone chimed. Bolting upright as though the fire alarm had been clanging in her ears, she groped for the phone. Her stomach dropped as she read the message.

> Elliott: Denise is pregnant.

CHAPTER 14
Elliott

Pregnant. Fucking pregnant. Granted if they'd had kids together, things would have been monumentally more complicated if they'd divorced. But one of the main reasons their marriage fell apart was because she'd said she didn't want kids—after marrying him under the false pretense of having fucking kids—and now she was having a goddamn kid.

As it turned out, she did want kids, just not with him.

The whistle blew on the ice, and he was reminded that they were at the barn, in the third period of a game, and they were barely clinging to a 1-0 lead against Cedar Rapids. Try as he might to care, he just couldn't find it in himself to give a flying fuck.

Fuck Cedar Rapids. Fuck hockey. Fuck everything.

Most of all, fuck fucking Denise and her fucking baby daddy.

Pregnant.

He ground his teeth together so tight his whole face ached. He'd put his entire life's plans on hold for her because she wasn't ready for kids—no, didn't even want kids. The kids she'd told him she wanted with him before he put a goddamn ring on her finger.

Pregnant.

Fucking pregnant.

"Coach?"

Shaking his head, he dismissed Linc with a wave. Not now. It's not a good time.

Seemingly getting the message, Linc barked a few orders at the team before slipping his mouth guard back in, throwing one last quizzical glance at Elliott, and skating back onto the ice.

Elliott knew he was being irrational. Nothing he said, did, or stewed on would change the fact he gave so much of his life to someone who was now shitting—once again—on everything they had.

But he couldn't stop his blood from boiling, he couldn't stop the clawing rage in his chest, or the bubbling blood under his skin.

The crowd falling deathly silent pulled his attention to the ice. Theo lay sprawled out at the feet of a de la Peña brother. Apollo, maybe, the number on his shirt wasn't in view.

On the big screen, the open ice check was repeated in slow motion. He winced. That had to hurt.

The de la Peña brother—it was Apollo after all—helped Theo to his unsteady feet to a smattering of applause from visibly concerned spectators. The check was good, clean, but hard, and Theo, all fifty pounds of the kid, had no chance.

Grant, a forward for the Snow Pirates, hurried across the ice to slip an arm under Theo's and help Apollo lead him off the ice. Apollo was almost as pale as Theo as he handed the rookie over to Linc and Brandon on the Snow Pirates' bench.

"I didn't mean to hurt him. I thought it was a clean hit."

Elliott cupped a hand over Apollo's shoulder pad and

squeezed. "It's all good, kid. It was a clean hit. Thanks for bringing him back."

"Of course." He turned to Theo who was getting checked over by a medic and hesitated.

Theo gave him a shaky thumbs up. "I'm fine, Apollo. For real."

He didn't look fine. He looked like he was gonna throw up on the medic's feet.

The Raccoon nodded, but he didn't seem convinced. His brother skated up behind him and handed him the broken pieces of Theo's stick which he in turn handed over the boards to Russell.

Linc gave him a firm nod as if to say everything was good between them before the de la Peña twins skated back out for the last few minutes of play in the game.

"You should be fine. Just a bit of a bone cruncher. But if you're still feeling woozy later, make sure you tell someone, okay?"

Theo nodded and gave a brittle smile. The hit had shaken him—it would have shaken anyone in the same position. Hell, he'd seen Austin Morgan, former enforcer for the Snow Pirates, take a hit from one of the de la Peña brothers and even he'd made his way back to the bench on shaky legs and looking a little green.

They were a force to be reckoned with.

And Elliott was jealous that they weren't *his* force. With the de la Peña boys guarding Theo's back like bulldogs, their team would be unstoppable.

Jealousy.

That was the ugly, bone-chilling feeling which had been weaving its cancerous way through his body all day. It was the bitter taste at the back of his mouth, the heavy weight in his stomach, and the sadness dragging him down.

How could he not be jealous? The woman he thought he'd be with forever was having a baby with another man.

"You okay?" Keeping one eye on the ice he turned to Theo who nodded.

"He hits like a wrecking ball."

Elliott nodded. "It's definitely not fun to get hit by the de la Peña brothers."

"You ever seen Doctor Strange, Coach?"

He nodded again, having no idea where this was going.

"Know when the bald chick yanks Doctor Strange out of his body?"

Elliott tried to contain a groan. "You mean the Sorceress Supreme?"

"Right. How I'm feeling right now is how I imagine that to feel."

Chuckling, Elliott turned his full attention back to the game as the seconds ticked down to the buzzer. He'd take a one-nil win over the Raccoons, and as long as Theo wasn't hurt, it was a decent game with a solid outcome. Another win in the books and another game closer to making the playoffs.

Stepping out of the rink, his stomach clenched at the sight of Denise standing next to his vehicle. "You've got to be fucking kidding me."

"Please, Lio? I'm sorry I lied about the house. But things are getting serious for me and now with the baby..." Her voice trailed off as she patted her stomach.

Was she really trying to manipulate him using her unborn child as leverage? Did the woman have no limits? How had he ever loved such an unscrupulous bitch?

"Can't you just give me the house and let us both move on?" Her saccharine sweet tone curdled his stomach. Was she delusional? Just *give* her the house? In her fucking dreams.

"You should go." He stepped around her and unlocked

the car. She grabbed the door with both hands, but he slipped into the driver's seat and jerked it from her grasp.

"Elliott, please. Be reasonable."

He guffawed. Reasonable. He'd been beyond reasonable, for years. Now he was just done. "Any further communications between us will be done through our lawyers, Dee. I'm changing my number, and if you ever show up like this again, I'll call the cops. Leave me the fuck alone."

Her face hardened and her eyes narrowed before she flipped him off and spun on her heel. As he drove in circles around the city in an attempt to clear his head, his stomach bubbled. How had he been so fucking stupid to be taken for a goddamn ride?

Was he really so gullible? So easy to manipulate? Part of him couldn't help but wonder if Denise was even really pregnant. It tore him apart to speculate, but he'd heard stories about narcissists who created a fictitious baby to manipulate something from their partners. Was that what Denise had done?

How could he be in the position where he was questioning his own ex-wife's motives, and doubting her on such a deep level? Did he even know her at all?

If only he'd kept his nerve and given the damn flowers to pregnant Clare back in high school. They'd have raised Cat together. Mason would have been their baby…

Except that wasn't how it worked, was it?

He thumped the steering wheel. "Fuuuuuck!"

With a deep breath, he said, "Hey, Siri. Call Clare."

Maybe talking to her would help.

Maybe seeing her, holding her, laughing with her would help ease the raw and festering wounds throughout his body.

He pointed the car toward her house and waited for the call to connect, tapping his fingers and thumbs on the wheel as he drove.

"Elliott?"

"Yeah, Clare, I—"

"Can I call you back? Now's... time." Her voice cracked with the line as she spoke.

"Clare? I can't hear you."

The light changed to red and he pumped the breaks, swearing under his breath.

"Sorry. Can you hear me now?" She paused. "Eli?"

She sounded tired, in fact, her voice held every ounce of exhaustion that he was feeling in each and every muscle and limb.

"Yeah. I was wondering—"

"Can I call you back? It's really not a good time."

A man's voice spoke in the background. Her asshole ex was there. What the fuck was he doing there at this time of night? It couldn't be anything good.

The rational part of his brain knew it was nothing untoward. He and Clare were together, she hated her ex with a passion, and rightfully so. She'd never take him back, not after the level of betrayal he'd inflicted upon her.

They'd both been burned by cheating exes—he knew without a second thought that she would never do that to him.

But a piece of him, a growing, angry, vibrating part of his heart wondered what that asshole needed to talk to her about that was so important that she dismissed Elliott to tend to. He rubbed his chest with the heel of his hand.

What the fuck did he have to do to be someone's priority for a goddamn change?

Clare

Clare had always thought that being a teenage mother with no friends in high school was the hardest moment of her life. However, watching Mason throw his belongings into a suitcase late at night while his asshole dad stood in the corner with a smirk on his face was, in fact, the hardest moment of her life.

Her heart was slowly splintering inside her body, and as much as she wanted to cry, she didn't want to guilt Mason into staying. He'd made his choice. And while it tore her apart, she didn't want him to feel bad for it, for leaving her.

He needed to find his own path and making him feel like shit for owning his tough AF decision would be a dick move. A Sperm Donor move.

She wasn't lowering herself to his level, nor was she going to hurt her child, no matter how much she, herself, was hurting.

Instead, she jerked up the elastic of her big girl panties with a snap, and helped her baby put his prized possessions in the bag.

"We can bring the rest over another time. But for now, just take what you need right away, okay?"

His sad eyes met hers as he nodded. "Sure, Mom. Thanks."

"Why don't you go downstairs and pack up some of your games?"

He left without a word, leaving Clare and The Sperm Donor to pack in silence. As she tucked his favorite Pokémon stuffy into the suitcase, The Sperm Donor grunted. "You know this probably wouldn't have happened if you weren't fucking around with the hockey coach, right?"

She wasn't going to rise to his bait. Ignoring him, she folded a sweater and placed it into the case.

"I know you're dating him. Mase said as much. Are you fucking him? It's been a while hasn't it? I bet you're fucking him."

Was that what this was about? The fact that she was finally getting some? Good. Let it bug the fuck out of him that she'd found someone who wasn't afraid to bend her over the back of the couch and give her a good fucking from time to time.

"It's not okay, Clare. Needing me to step up and help out with our son because you're too busy fucking some deadbeat to be his mother. It's not okay, you hear me? I won't stand for it anymore. I'm done. I'm drawing a line."

Huh. And just what exactly would he do about it? Folding her arms, she narrowed her eyes at him, glaring. "Are you threatening me?"

His brows twitched, but his face didn't give anything away. "I'm simply saying that Mason moving in with me is just the beginning. And that if you're continually too busy with your boyfriend to take care of your son, perhaps I should file for sole custody."

Her jaw dropped open for a split second before she composed herself. Would he really declare all-out war over the fact that she was moving on with her life? That she was happy with someone else?

"You cheated on me, remember? You left me. For your secretary no less, like a cliché from a goddamn fucking movie. So what is this? You don't want me so no one else can have me?" She deliberately kept her voice low so Mason wouldn't hear her tearing his father a new asshole.

He grunted again and turned his attention back to packing. "We'll see who wins."

"And that's it, right there." She jabbed an accusing finger his direction. "This isn't a game to me. This is my life, my son. I'll do what's best for him. Not what wins me the most points." She couldn't bear the sight of his smug fucking face for a moment longer.

She charged down the stairs, stomping on each one as she descended, it was childish, but she didn't give a shit. It was her house. Sure, it was falling down around her ears, but it was something no one could take away from her, no matter how hard they tried. She found Mason in the kitchen with an over heaped spoonful of ice cream mid-way to his mouth and a sheepish grin on his face.

"Want a bite?"

She shook her head. She needed something stronger, something much stronger, but she only had a bottle of wine in the house. What she wouldn't give for some raspberry and Limoncello cocktails and a couple of baskets of mozzarella sticks about now.

Maybe later.

But first she had to get Mason packed up and off to his father's, then she needed to call Elliott back. He'd sounded upset, but she only had the bandwidth to deal with one crisis at a time. Mason came first.

Her kids always came first. No matter what.

And right now, her heart being surreptitiously ripped from her chest by the child she grew and birthed then being stepped on by the size thirteens of his asshole father, was more than enough for her to deal with.

She dragged a hand through her tangled hair. She also needed a shower. Had it been two days? Three? Why was everything so damned hard?

Twenty minutes later, Mason had his earthly possessions in-hand and arrogant Sperm Donor was waving a cheery goodbye. Clare closed the door and sank to the floor, finally letting the tears fall that had been threatening all evening.

Why couldn't she catch a break?

She was a good person, she gave what she could to charity, she paid her taxes, and she'd never committed a crime in her entire life—except that one time she ran a red light on accident. But just one time.

And while she wasn't the best mother in the world, she made sure that every single day she was the best she could be.

Why wasn't it enough? Why was nothing ever enough?

She cradled her head in her hands as she cried. The real question, the one she'd faced every day of her damned life since the pregnancy test had told her she was pregnant with Cat, was why was *she* never enough?

The more she cried, the further she slipped, and by the time she pulled her numb ass from the cold floor tiles and made her way into the kitchen, she was numb.

Elliott had abandoned her. Cat's dad had abandoned her. Mason's dad had abandoned her. Her parents were abandoning her to move to Florida. At some point everyone left her. She was broken, unlovable, unworthy of everything.

There was no way in hell Elliott truly wanted her, and even if he did, she didn't deserve him.

Her chest ached. Her high school boyfriend had left her, Elliott had left her, Cat's father had left her, and now Mason had left her. Why would she give her heart back to Elliott when he was only going to leave her all over again? Just like he had before, just like everyone else did.

It was only a matter of time.

CHAPTER 15
Clare

Elliott: Call me when you're free.

Clare tucked the phone into her back pocket and went back to scrubbing the inside of the toilet bowl. She'd seen some kind of chemical cocktail on social media where a person used what must have been eight full bottles of various cleaning supplies to clean their freakin' toilet.

The woman on the clip layered the different colors of cleaners over the top of one another to make a vibrant pattern. But as pretty as all the colors were, nothing beat a bit of elbow grease and some Clorox to get the bathroom sparkly clean.

Two days. She'd managed to avoid Elliott for an entire two days without telling him why. He hadn't called her, or texted much, but he had let her know—twice—that he wanted to talk whenever she had a minute.

But she couldn't bring herself to pick up the phone.

Mason was gone, Catriona was staying with friends—yet again. She was trying not to get too in her head about the fact that her kid was spending way more time with her friends than she was at home.

She'd be moving out in a couple months anyway, but her ever naïve and hopeful self had thought she'd have more time with her before she flew the coop.

Clare was alone.

She'd cleaned the whole house twice over in two days. Thanks to half a bottle of Fabuloso, she could see her reflection in every floor tile, and if she was so inclined she could eat her breakfast, lunch, and dinner off each of the toilets in the house.

Standing up and blowing at her hair again, she pulled off her gloves, tucked the cleaning supplies back under the sink, and washed her hands.

Next up was food. Now that she'd cleaned the kitchen to within an inch of its life, it was time to trash it again by making a shit ton of comfort food. Why did people do that? Clean up before making a mess?

And wasn't that how every grown-ass adult dealt with their problems? Bleaching the shit out of their house and then cooking everything in the pantry?

There was nothing in the world that couldn't be solved by Lizzo. Literally nothing. That queen had a song for every occasion. So, cranking up *About Damn Time* to maximum socially acceptable volume, she hauled out her baking supplies, borrowed one of Cat's TikTok crowns, and got to work.

Blueberry muffins—check. Double batch of chocolate brownies—check, check.

Fuck that Sperm Donor asshole. While it wasn't a competition, she was going to make sure the freezer was stocked with all of Mason's favorite foods, so when he did come to visit, she wasn't panic baking a bunch of shit. Just call her Efficient Mom.

Okay, so her superhero name needed some work, but she

felt a deep satisfaction when she managed to get her shit together and hold it there for any length of time.

Organization was her forte. Lists, meal plans, color-coordinated spreadsheets and batch cooking like a mothafuckin' boss bitch. But with her job, two kids, and a hockey schedule, she never really felt like she was on top of, well, anything.

Zucchini bread with walnuts—check. Two loaves of chocolate chip banana bread—check, check.

She was on fire—and if the kitchen got much hotter, the house would probably be, too. But she didn't stop until she'd exhausted every egg, stick of butter, and most of her flour and sugar supplies too.

Two dozen snickerdoodles, and a dozen chocolate chip peanut butter cookies took up cooling racks on the counter, a pot of chicken and wild rice soup simmered on the stove, and the largest pan of Meemaw's lasagna cooled on the breakfast bar.

The dishwasher was on its second cycle, and the kitchen didn't look at all like she'd scrubbed around the faucet with a toothbrush only hours before. Instead, a thin film of flour coated just about every surface, and she couldn't quite tell if the haze around the room was smoke coming from the oven, or a haze of baking supplies from Hurricane Avoidance.

Sweat trickled down her neck and face, into her eyes, and she swiped it away with the heel of her hand.

The front door burst open and the distinct sound of a bag falling onto tiles met her ears. "I'm back." Cat wasn't due back for another night, and her voice was...flat. Or something.

Her Mom-dar—radar for moms—went straight to high alert.

"I have snacks." It was the only thing she could have said that could lure her daughter into the kitchen rather than skulking straight upstairs and hiding in her room.

Was it fair to bribe her kid with a sugar high in a bid to find out what was going on with her? Probably not.

Did she feel in the least bit guilty about it? Fuck no.

Cat made a beeline for the fridge, grabbing the gallon of chocolate milk from the door and closing it with a soft thud. She unscrewed the top and the milk was halfway to her lips when Clare pointed at the cupboard where the glasses lived.

Her kids were fucking animals.

"Don't be gross. Use a glass."

Cat flicked her glare between the bottle in her hand and Clare, once, twice, and on the third time she must have decided it wasn't worth the battle and reached to get a glass with a sigh.

"Did you have Betty Crocker over for the afternoon, or what?"

Clare stepped back from the counter and wiped her hands on her apron. "Kinda looks that way, doesn't it?" She shrugged. "I had free time today, so I thought I'd fill the freezer."

"With all our favorite snacks?" Cat arched a brow and reached forward to wipe something off Clare's face with her thumb.

"I had the ingredients...and the space in the freezer..."

Cat's brow crept further up her forehead.

"I'd rather make stuff you guys will eat when you're home. No point in making shit that's gonna live in the freezer and make friends with the frost mites." She smiled, but Cat remained sullen. "What can I get for you?" She grabbed a side plate and waved it around.

"I can attest the chocolate brownies are every bit as delicious as they look and smell. Perfectly fudgy in the middle with a fine crisp outer shell. And don't ask me how I know, I'm not proud of my behavior."

That made Catriona's lips twitch ever so slightly. "Sold. I'll take two."

Clare picked up two edge pieces—because her daughter was a weirdo who preferred them to the center pieces—and as she passed the plate to Cat, she paused. "Wanna talk about it?"

Tears sprung into her daughter's eyes and she shook her head. "Bribe first, then information."

She wasn't born yesterday. Cat knew exactly how her mom worked. And Clare could respect wanting to feed her feelings before talking it out. With a nod, she pulled the vanilla ice cream from the freezer and heaped a dollop on top of Cat's brownies.

Between mouthfuls of chewy brownies, Cat narrowed her eyes and pointed her spoon at Clare. "You can't lose your shit."

Hackles activated. Mom-poker-face initiated. "No promises. But I'll do my best."

After another bite, Catriona nodded. "I'll take it." But she fell silent, dipping her head and staring blankly at the plate of food in front of her. Was she trying to figure out how to tell her whatever the hell it was she had to say? Or was that the end of the conversation?

Was she taking drugs? Had her behavior changed? Was she dropping out of school? Was she pregnant? Wait, was she having sex? Shit. Fuck. What. The. Fuck? Sure, she'd offered her protection, but she didn't think she'd actually use it. Or maybe she just didn't want to think about her using it. She shuddered.

She wanted to grab her darling child by the shoulders and scream "tell mcccceeee" but she gnawed on the inside of her cheek. Trying to funnel patience from somewhere deep inside her tummy, she unloaded the dishwasher to keep her hands busy instead.

"Catriona?"

She held up a finger, took a deep breath, and when she lifted her head to meet Clare's eyes, tears trickled down her face. Curiosity on momentary pause, Clare crossed the short distance to the breakfast bar and wrapped her beloved baby in a mom-hug.

Those kinds of hugs that hit differently. Those hugs that squeeze you back together when you feel like you're coming apart at the seams and you have no idea how to stop the free fall.

"Whatever it is, it'll be okay baby girl."

Cat shook her head against her shoulder. "I should have listened to you."

Her stomach tightened. About what? Drugs? Boys? School? Sex? She needed a little more to work with. Her daughter was the personification of click-bait and Clare needed the below-the-fold detail.

Cat sat upright, pushing herself away from Clare's shoulder and sniffed. "I've been dating...someone."

The way she mumbled her words and wouldn't meet Clare's gaze was a sure sign that it was probably not someone Clare would approve of. "Okay...? That's it? That's the whole story?"

Teenage glare: intensified.

Dang. She had it down pat.

"You already know that's not the whole story."

Clare nodded. "I do. But I also can't help you if you don't tell me what's going on, and I can't hear you if you mumble into your dessert."

Cat rolled her eyes. She was a foot stamp away from the trifecta of teenage tantrums. When her nostrils stopped flaring, she took another bite. "I was dating Chad."

Chad.

By some serendipitous or divine intervention, Clare had managed to keep Chad away from Catriona for her entire childhood education to date. With only a short time left before graduation, she'd fallen at the final hurdle.

Fucking Chad.

The all-star high school quarter back who was reportedly using performance enhancing drugs. The student who flunked damn near every class but no one seemed to give two shits because he was some kind of sports god. The asshole who'd broken the hearts of almost every one of Cat's friends over the years.

Please no, not Chad.

"I can feel your judgment, Mom."

She held her hands up. "No judgment. Maybe you're pickin' up my stench though. I really need a shower after all this." She sniffed her armpit before sweeping a hand through the air above all the food, but Cat's face remained serious.

"I thought he'd changed."

If wishing made it so.

"I thought he was different."

Didn't every woman? But in large part they were all the same. Once a lying piece of shit, always a lying piece of shit.

"I thought he wanted to be better. To do better. For me." She sniffed again and wiped her trickling tears on the back of her forearm.

Clare reached over the counter and tugged a Kleenex from the box.

"What did he do?" Attempting to keep her voice level didn't seem to be working, but if Catriona had noticed, she didn't show it. "Did he cheat on you?"

"Worse."

What was worse than cheating? Rape? Fuck. If that kid laid a hand on Cat without her consent she'd string him up by his dick and cut off his balls with a rusty knife.

"Did he hurt you?"

Cat put her spoon onto the plate and shook her head.

"Not physically. He's using again. He said he stopped. He promised he'd stop, but..."

Relief doused the raging fire in Clare's chest, and a wave of pride washed over her. Her baby was making good choices, even if she'd made questionable ones at first.

"I caught him. I thought he'd stopped. I mean, he might have, but he's back using and I don't want to be around that, Mom. I really don't."

She gave Cat another big squeeze. "While I'm not thrilled you were dating that intergalactic asshole, I'm very proud of you for stepping away from that shit. You have a bright future ahead of you, and I don't want it shit on by fucking *Chad*."

Cat nodded. "It just hurts, you know?"

She knew all too well.

Another tidal wave of sobbing and tears erupted from Cat and Clare watched helplessly as she dealt with her first asshole ex-boyfriend, her first heartbreak, her first betrayal.

Getting to nineteen without having a broken heart experience was pretty good going as far as relationships went, but it still tore her apart to watch her baby cry over a dumb fucking boy. Let alone one who didn't deserve her kid in the least.

Fucking Chad.

"Is there anything I can do?"

Another sniff, a lip quiver, and wide, sad, and watery eyes filled with gut-wrenching sadness. "Just don't say you told me so. I'm well aware." Cat picked up her plate and dragged her tongue through the brownie-ice cream debris.

Clare's hand shot out and smacked Cat's forearm. "Gross."

"We're in the privacy of our own home, Mom. If I wanna lick the plate, then I'm sorry, but I'mma lick the motherfuckin' plate." She pointed the almost clean plate at Clare. "And you can't even judge me. I live with you, remember?"

She snorted. The kid had a point.

"I'm going upstairs to cry it out to angsty music for a little bit."

When she reached out to touch her, Cat shrugged her off, sending a pang through her chest into her heart. "I'll be okay, Mom. I just need a little time."

The black cloud of sadness hanging over her kid grew darker as she trudged out of the kitchen, but a double chime forced her not to dwell as both the oven timer and the doorbell rang at the same time.

Fuck. She hurried to pull the pan of chicken pasta bake from the oven and place it on a trivet before bolting through the house to answer the door.

Oven gloves still in hand, disheveled, wrapped in an apron that probably had more food on it than her kitchen counters, she answered the door.

"Kenzie?" Clare stepped out onto the porch and peered around her next door neighbor.

If that asshole ex-husband of Kenzie's had made a reappearance, Clare was more than prepared to Carrie Underwood the shit out of his fancy pants car.

"Is everything okay?"

"Yes, ma'am. I wanted to bring you these." She handed over a bouquet of flowers. "To say thanks, for... you know..." She jerked a thumb over her shoulder toward her house. "Rescuing me."

"Psssh. I don't need thanks—us single ladies have to stick together, right?" She paused. "Plus, you've already said thank you, Kenz. A couple of times now." She fell quiet, hoping Kenzie would fill the silence.

Her beautiful, southern belle neighbor's pale cheeks flushed rosy. Considering she had been at prom with Austin Morgan—of *the* Minnesota Morgan fame—Clare was pretty sure she wasn't a single lady any longer.

Good for her. Eli had nothing but good things to say about his former player Austin and Kenzie deserved the world.

When she didn't turn to leave, Clare narrowed her eyes. "Was there something else?"

Kenzie twisted her hands in front of her and chewed on the inside of her lip. "It's not my place."

"And yet here you are." She winked, though not feeling light hearted and heaved in a breath. Elliott. It had to be. That was the only other potential connection she could think of, considering her next-door neighbor was a physiotherapist for the Snow Pirates. That or she was there to complain about Lizzo singing too loudly in Clare's kitchen all morning.

It could probably have gone either way.

She stepped back and waved an arm. "Do you wanna come in?"

With a small shake of her head, she took a step back. "Lincoln mentioned yesterday that Coach Swift is...uh...out of sorts. And I know you're...um..." She rolled her eyes to the heavens and whispered something to herself which sounded a lot like "this is so awkward," and the apples of her cheeks darkened further.

"I know you're friends with him, and I know he's more than entitled to a private life but if it's his father's health, or something he needs support from the team on. Well..." She dropped her hands to her sides with a clap. "We're here, I guess is what I'm trying to say. Linc wants him to know the guys are there for him."

As sweet as it was that the team had Eli's back, he would be horrified to know that they'd even noticed he was struggling, never mind that Kenzie had knocked on Clare's door to talk about it.

It wasn't her story to tell, and the guilt at not calling Elliott back was more stifling than the overbearing heat wafting from her kitchen.

"Thank you, Kenzie. He's lucky to have you." She squeezed the woman's elbow. "All of you. I'm sure it was just a bad day."

Kenzie cringed.

"Week. A bad week. And he'll be back to his not-quite-as-bad self in no time."

Kenzie's nostrils flared as she sucked in a deep breath and gave an uncertain nod. "I hope so."

She offered a smile. "I'll talk to him."

That seemed to ease Kenzie's worries a little more. "Okay, thank you."

"No problem. You want a cookie?"

"Please. The smells coming from your kitchen have been permeating my house all freakin' morning and driving me crazy. It all smells so darn delicious."

Once Kenzie had a stack of cookies and a serving of pasta bake bundled in her arms, she waggled her fingers goodbye and walked across the yard to her house leaving Clare with literally no other methods of procrastination.

It was time to call Elliott.

CHAPTER 16
Elliott

"I was just about to call you." Under flushed cheeks, wild hair, a brown smudge on her left cheekbone that he hoped was chocolate, and an apron that probably needed to be burned rather than washed, Clare answered the door with an uncertain smile.

"I figured you couldn't really avoid me any longer if I just up and landed on your doorstep."

She had the decency to wince at his words. "I've had stuff going on."

Didn't everyone?

Stepping back, she waved him into the house. Smiling pictures of Mason and Catriona hung in the hallway, but few pictures of Clare adorned the walls.

He was only a few feet through the door before his mouth watered and a myriad of smells accosted his nose. "Smells delicious in here."

Clare shrugged and led the way into the kitchen. "I had some time so I thought I'd make some things."

Holy baked goods, Batman. "Some things? Don't you mean all the things?"

She laughed but it was brittle. "Coffee?"

"As long as I can have something from this selection to go with it."

"Sure." Her smile was weak, her shoulders curled forward, and it looked like she carried the weight of the world on her back.

"Mason moved in with his dad."

Ah. Shit. That would account for the sadness radiating from her every pore, the production line in the kitchen, and the faint undertone of bleach he'd picked up as they walked through the house. "That explains..." He waved an arm. "This place is pretty clean. I guess that's an upside to living alone."

Her face fell, then her features hardened, and for a split second he wondered if she was going to throw the brimming cup of scalding coffee in her hand at his dumbass head. Before he could backpedal, she opened her mouth and spat her own attack at him.

"I guess it's not fair of me to expect you to understand when you don't have kids."

He gritted his teeth. They were a barb a piece. They fell into an uncomfortable silence, each stewing over what the other had said. Or at least that's what he assumed from the cautious glances and angry sips she took from her mug.

Who knew you could drink coffee angrily?

While she was right, it still stung, especially because Denise was... He couldn't even think the word.

By the time he'd reached the bottom of his mug, they still hadn't spoken again. He knew one thing for sure though, Clare Reynolds could make a better snickerdoodle than anyone else in the whole entire world. Even Mom.

He groaned as he took another bite, washing it down with the last mouthful of his coffee. She pinned him with a hard stare. Maybe she'd poisoned the cookies. If she had, at least he'd die happy. Best cookies ever.

"Was there something you needed...or...?"

Was she really kicking him out already? Man, she was pissed. "I just wanted to know if you were still up for our cooking class tomorrow night."

He could almost see the *oh shit, that's tomorrow night?* flicker across her face before she composed herself.

"Oh. Yeah. Absolutely." She sipped her drink.

"Okay."

"Okay."

That was that, then. He stood up and tucked his hands in his pockets. If he didn't he might reach out to grab her and kiss her until she wasn't mad at him anymore. "I should probably go."

She rose to her feet and untied the apron around her waist, then pulled it over her head. Tossing it onto the table, she sighed. "Sure."

"That's it?"

With a shrug, she spread her hands wide. "What else do you want, Eli?"

He closed the space between them, their noses touched, and her tits brushed against his chest with every breath.

"This isn't a good idea." She stepped back, but he followed. He couldn't bear her being out of arm's reach.

"Why not?"

"We're both upset." Her eyes flicked to his lips, and the flush that was spreading up her neck settled in her cheeks. "We both have stuff going on."

He nodded. They did.

"Cat's upstairs."

That gave him pause. When they'd last spoken, Clare had said Cat wasn't due back for another couple days. Something must have gone belly up to bring the kid back home. He wanted to ask, he wanted to be the caring boyfriend she needed him to be, but his skin was on fire and he needed her touch to put out the flames.

They stood silently staring at each other, the air around them sizzling with frustrations and lust. His heart beat loudly in his ears, and he wanted nothing more than to fuck her until they both felt better.

Instead, he took a step back and nodded. "Okay. It's not the time. I get it." It wasn't the time. Angry fucking never fixed anything. He knew that. It didn't stop his whole body from wanting her in his arms, though.

He walked another two feet back, but this time she closed the gap. As she nibbled on her lip, she gripped his shirt and tugged him toward her. Walking backward, she stretched his shirt out until he caved and followed her into the laundry room with slow steps.

Talk about confusing. She was mad at him, not talking to him, but she was dragging him into the room off the kitchen with fire in her eyes.

"We need to be quick." She was already unbuttoning his pants.

He nodded, slipping his thumbs into the waist of his jeans and shucking them down past his ass. While her signals were confusing, he wasn't going to turn down the chance to fuck her.

"I can do quick." In truth he was afraid he'd end up being too quick for her. He ached to be inside her, to lose himself in her.

As she wiggled her yoga pants down her calves with one hand, she pointed the other at him. "And quiet."

He snickered. "I'm not the loud one in this relationship."

She curled her outstretched finger back into her fist and made an 'O' shape with her mouth. "Point taken." Bracing her hands on either side of her body, she jumped up onto the washer and spread her legs, reaching out grabby hands at him, her fingertips skimming his nipples sending shivers to his toes.

He paused. He needed to give her a chance to change her mind. "You sure about this?"

She licked her lips, narrowing her eyes. "You don't want angry sex with me?"

"I want every sex with you."

She laughed and covered her mouth with her hands, her eyes flaring wide. "Shh!" She flapped a hand at him. "Don't make me laugh."

He schooled his face. "Because you don't want Cat to hear?" He had dropped his voice to a whisper.

"No. Well, yes, I don't want her to hear, but I also wanna stay mad at you."

Her pants and panties dangled from her left ankle. Wait. Women wore panties with leggings? Weren't they basically pj pants? Shit. Did women wear panties with pj pants?

It wasn't the time to get into it, but it was something he'd ask her about when there weren't as many "I hate you" vibes still pouring off of her.

"You don't wanna kick them all the way off?"

She grabbed his collar and pulled him to her. "No. It's faster to get one leg back on than both in case we're interrupted."

Fair point. She'd clearly had sex with the kids at home before. Ugh. Yeah. No. He didn't want to think about that. Especially since he knew no one had ever treated her the way she'd deserved to be treated between the sheets. Or on top of the washer for that matter. He grinned.

"What are you waiting for Eli? Do you need a map? A neon sign?" She scooted her ass to the very edge of the machine and pointed to her pussy. "Get inside me."

"Wow, Ceecee. I shall compare thee to a summer's day."

"Fuck the summer's day. Make me come." She grabbed his

dick and pumped twice, sending all rational thought out the window.

He tossed her a salute. "Yes, ma'am." He guided his tip to her entrance and dragged it through her arousal, noting the softening of her features, of her muscles, and the small sigh that escaped her as he edged himself inside her.

Fuck. She felt like heaven. "Fast and quiet, right?"

The fire in her eyes intensified as she nodded. Curling an arm around her waist, he sank all the way into her with a quick push. They'd both probably regret not talking out their issues and instead resorting to a fast bang on the washing machine, but in the moment, she felt too good to argue with.

He grunted as he slid out and rammed into her again. Her ass squeaked against the shiny, white top of the machine as he thrust. She was stuck to the damned thing, making it difficult for him to do anything quickly.

She giggled. "Maybe I should have left my panties on so I'd glide against the machine instead of my ass cheeks getting stuck to it."

Softening his knees, he bent a little before wrapping her legs around his waist and picking her up. She quieted herself against his shoulder, burying her face into his shirt with a muffled moan as he loosened his grip just enough to slide her down his body so he was balls deep in her.

He turned them both around and pressed her back against the wall, pumping faster and faster. She threw her head back, wincing when it connected with the wall.

"Shit." She grunted and crammed her finger in her mouth, biting down on it like it was going to keep her silent.

It only served to spur him on. He fucked her harder and harder with each thrust, intent on making her come undone around his cock. He slipped his hand between them and fingered her slick clit as she bounced eagerly on his dick.

She clenched her teeth.

"Come for me, Clare."

She shook her head. Stubborn, stubborn woman. He drove into her again and again. Slaps of bare skin meeting bare skin, and the quiet grunts and heaving breaths echoed around the small room as she inched up and down the wall.

"I said come for me." His words came out on a low growl through gritted teeth. He was so close to just letting go in her tight, hot pussy, but as a matter of personal pride he always wanted Clare to come first.

She sank her teeth into her bottom lip and grinned at him. Another head shake. His fingers glided around her clit in quickening circles and her body started to tense and tremble.

He had her.

"You sure you're not going to come for me?"

She nodded, but it was jerky and her smug smile wavered.

Keeping the pace of plunging his dick into her as well as the rhythm of rolling circles over her clit got trickier the closer he got to his own orgasm.

"Come." Thrust. "For." Thrust. "Me."

She burst apart, tingling all over. Her nails squeezed into his skin through his shirt, and if he wasn't mistaken, she had bit down on her lip so hard she'd drawn blood—but he didn't stop.

He rode her through her orgasm, not easing off, not changing his speed, not going any more gently with her. He pounded her with every ounce of determination he had. Just as he crested the final wave into his own release, she tensed around him again. He wasn't sure if it was still the first climax, or if she was coming again, but he didn't care. It didn't matter.

He held her, pumping her until every drop of his cum was inside her, and until her body went soft. It was only when she slid down his body and planted her feet on the floor that he realized they hadn't even kissed the whole time.

Cupping her jaw, he tipped her head back and descended

on her mouth with fervor. He poured all of himself into her. Every ounce of his love, his pain, his frustration, and she met him thrust for thrust with her tongue as she gripped his shirt in a balled fist.

She flattened her palm against his chest and pushed him back before touching her fingertips to her lips. "You need to go." She kissed him again. "Or that's going to happen again."

And that was a bad thing? Sure, he'd need a minute or two to recover—maybe five—but he was only too happy to fuck her again. He spoke through their sloppy kisses. "I'm totally okay with that."

She shook her head, making their noses brush against each other. "I'm not. And I have cold jizz trickling down my thighs. I gotta clean up." She pushed his chest again. "And you've gotta let me."

He nodded, but he wasn't convinced. He didn't give a fuck if the whole laundry room was covered in their bodily fluids—he wanted to be inside her again, and his half-mast dick twitched in agreement.

"Are we still cooking tomorrow?"

She rolled her eyes. "Of course we are. I need to learn how to make risotto." She paused. "And the chocolate thing. I promised Mason I'd make it for him when he's here next. Plus...I might want to see you, too." She winked at him and the tension in his chest loosened just enough to take a deep breath.

He'd take "might." It meant he wasn't out of the game altogether—at least not yet.

The cooking class was a three-hour deal downtown in Minneapolis. And somehow in those three hours, they were going to make a three-course meal. Roasted butternut squash risotto, crusted salmon with cheesy scalloped potatoes and asparagus, and a chocolate cake thing with a molten middle for dessert.

At the time Dad had given him the gift it sounded like a great idea. But standing in the industrial kitchen with five other couples and a very attractive male instructor at the front of the room, he was starting to think perhaps it was a little overambitious—especially considering he couldn't even boil an egg.

It didn't help that things with Clare were still...frosty. While he'd put their spat—was that even what it was?—behind him, she seemed to still be stewing in her emotions.

She had seemed guarded when he picked her up, guiding his lips to her cheek instead of letting him kiss her on the lips. Her conversation had been polite, perfectly nice, but he knew her better than she even knew herself, and she was holding back. Did he though? He was questioning what was going on in her mind, and he'd spent the last twenty years away from her.

Was he losing her? Or was she just taking some time to adjust to the huge changes happening in her life?

"Can you pass the squash, please, Eli?" Her expectant eyes suggested he'd been in a world of his own and missed something. "I need to peel it and get it into the oven to roast."

Roast. Right. They were making food. He handed it to her with a smile. Maybe she just missed having Mason around the house. Maybe if he kept her busy enough... No, she'd still feel his absence.

Distractions weren't going to counteract the feelings of acute loss at her son having moved out. If it wouldn't have drawn questions from everyone in the room, he'd have smacked himself.

"How is the team doing?" She sliced the nubby end off the squash and went to work with the peeler.

He nodded. Safe territory. The team. Work. He could handle that. "Good. Better than good. It seems we finally found our vibe and we're set to make the playoffs."

Her smile was genuine, warm, and he felt it in his whole body like a shot of serotonin straight to his soul. "I'm glad. Theo took Mason skating the other day. He really does seem like a nice enough boy."

"He's finding his feet for sure."

She paused slicing the squash. "Cat broke up with some douche nozzle she'd been seeing behind my back. I'd say I can't wait for her to get to college but it's only going to get worse."

She wasn't wrong. Cat was a stunning young woman, smart, funny, and from what Clare had told him, she was popular and had a lot of friends. Hell, half of his hockey players probably wanted to date her after her appearance at prom.

"I can have some of the team watch her back if she comes to the U if you'd like?" Those already in relationships so they weren't tempted to try to bed her themselves anyway.

He sliced the end off an onion and pulled the skin off with both hands before attempting to dice it. "And by 'watch her back' I—of course—mean beat the ever living shit out of anyone who goes near her. And if she ends up somewhere else... I know people."

How did people make chopping an onion look so easy? Tears streamed down his face and from the mess of onion in front of him it looked like Mason had cut it up with a dull skate.

Not that he could even see it through the welling tears.

Was it an extra-terrestrial onion? Did it have super onion strength? That had to be why he was crying like a baby, right?

Clare chortled, moving closer to him. "Here." She covered his hand with hers. "Tuck your fingers so we don't end up at the ER. Guide the onion through the knife."

How the hell did you guide the onion through the knife? Wait. She was moving the food, not the knife. That had to be what she meant, right? As opposed to moving the knife back and forth?

He had to admit—albeit reluctantly—that her way was easier than Hulk-smashing the onion with the knife like he had been doing.

"I think Dad was playing a joke on me when he got me this *experience*. I'm shit in the kitchen."

Clare bumped him with her hip. "You're not...shit."

Out of the corner of his eye he caught her rolling her lips and turning her face away.

"Lies. You..." He pointed the knife at her before going back to chopping. "You're even laughing at me. Laughing at the afflicted, Clare Reynolds. I thought you were better than that."

She snorted. "No, you didn't. And being a lazy asshat in the kitchen isn't an affliction."

He paused his knife. "It's not?"

"Unfortunately not. So I can laugh at you all I want. Jesus, Eli, it's like you've never held a knife before."

She wasn't entirely wrong. He did have a tendency to lean on his parents for the food part of his days before everything went to shit. And Denise—for all her flaws—was an exceptional cook.

Now that he lived alone, he avoided the kitchen because cooking for one was such a pain in the ass when every recipe under the sun was written for two fucking people. It was just another reminder of how he'd fucked up his life and ended up alone.

Clare made the class fun, and she took the same care with each stage of the process that she did with everything else in her life. By the time they got to the entrées, she'd thawed enough that they were both more at ease.

"Is now a bad time to tell you that I'm not a big fish eater?" Her stage whisper drew a raised eyebrow from the instructor, but that didn't faze her.

"What about little fish?" He picked up the plate of salmon and inched it toward her.

"That was terrible."

It was. But her giggle was worth it. When they sat down to try the salmon course, the teacher stupidly opened a bottle of Sauvignon Blanc which only made them even more obnoxious and giddy.

The dude, who Elliott was convinced kept making eyes at Clare, just ignored them and occasionally passed by their station with a look of contempt and derision. Whether it was at their behavior, or the mess building up around their meal, who could tell?

Elliott speared a piece of flaky salmon onto his fork and cupped the space beneath it as he guided it to Clare's mouth. "Trust me. It's delicious. Not too...fishy."

With a smile she accepted the mouthful and chewed for a few seconds before groaning. "You're right. That's tasty. The parmesan breadcrumb topping is just..." She gave a chef's kiss, drawing another eye roll from the teacher.

Mercifully, Clare and Elliott weren't the worst, or even the most disruptive couple in the room. A tiny, pixie-looking woman with short, bright red hair in the far back corner seemed to be an even more disastrous cook than Elliott. So much so that she managed to set her salmon on fire.

Just enough to ruin the couple's entrées, but not enough

to set off the fire alarm, or trigger the fire suppression system. The acrid stench of smoke hung in the air and clung to their hair and clothes. It was going to take some scrubbing to get off.

Clare had already shoveled half of her cheesy potatoes in her face and was making light work of the bacon wrapped asparagus.

"This feels like such a fancy dinner." She grinned as she chomped the end of a stalk of asparagus.

The instructor clapped his hands at the front of the room and announced that the class was getting away from them. Understatement of the century. The couple to their right had somehow abandoned the idea of cheesy scalloped potatoes and with the bacon from their asparagus had made bacon cheese fries.

Bacon fucking cheese fries. At a fancy cooking class.

He wasn't sure whether to be impressed and high-five them or slap them upside the head. But either way, he definitely wanted bacon cheese fries.

He lowered his lips to Clare's ear, enjoying the shiver that passed through her. "Are you still a heathen who eats her bacon cheese fries with ketchup?"

She folded her arms. "Damn straight, you ranch weirdo."

He picked up the pre-measured chocolate and butter and tipped it into the double boiler.

"Okay, fine. There's a chance my ketchup might be the anomaly."

"Oh?" He wasn't making eye contact with her. If she was admitting she was wrong about something he was going to let her and quietly enjoy it in aaaaall its freakin' glory.

"When I went to community college, they all thought it was weird too. Ranch all round. Not a single person ate them with ketchup like I do."

"Yes!" He fist pumped and shook his ass. "What was that?"

He cupped a hand around his ear and leaned it closer to her. "Was that the sound of you telling me I'm right?"

She shoved him. "You wish. You're just *all* wrong." She planted her hands on her hips and jerked her chin at the counter. "Keep going, you're doing just fine."

When the class finished, he kissed her by the car. She tasted of dark chocolate and strawberries, and they both smelled like they'd been at a local BBQ for the night.

As they parted, her phone went crazy in her pocket. Chime after chime after chime.

She patted the back pockets of her jeans, searched the pockets of her jacket, and eventually produced the still wailing phone from the bottom of her purse. His stomach hardened and his blood ran cold. There was only one reason someone's phone made that much noise and it was never a good one.

Something was wrong.

With trembling hands she pressed the phone to one ear and her finger in the other. The color drained from her face as she listened to a message.

"It's Mason. We need to go to the hospital."

CHAPTER 17
Clare

Elliott wasted no time herding Clare into the car and setting off for the hospital. She scrolled through her texts and listened to the escalating—verging on abusive—voicemails from her ex that waited for her as they rode in tense silence.

What did it say about them that two times they had spent time together they'd ended up in a panicked drive to the hospital? It kind of felt like punishment.

From what she gathered from both Catriona and The Sperm Donor's messages, Mason had fallen on the ice and hurt his wrist. He cried in the background of the voice messages The Sperm Donor left, and her heart shattered as she listened to her little boy whimpering in pain.

Fuck.

What the hell had she been thinking? As a single mom, checking she had cell phone coverage wherever she went was hardwired into her very existence. Her kids came first. Always. No exceptions.

Twisting the strap of her purse in her lap, her knee bounced as they approached a red light. They needed to hurry the fuck up, her baby needed her. And if she was honest with herself, she also needed reassurance that he needed her too, or at least that he was still speaking to her after she'd abandoned him when he needed her.

What kind of mother went off and had a blast drinking wine and cooking chocolate fucking cake while her kiddo was in pain in the hospital? As she scrolled through her messages, she paused her thumb on the screen—Cat mentioned in one of her texts that Mason might even need surgery.

Clare's stomach sloshed, and she grimaced. Surgery. Her littlest baby. Double fuck.

Side eyeing Elliott, she felt sick. How did some people have it all? The dating, the career, the kids… How did they have everything and yet not fuck up anything?

If she hadn't been on the stupid date with Eli, she would have been there for the first call. Hell, if she hadn't been dating Elliott at all, Mason might never have moved in with his dad either.

"Say what you're thinking, Clare." His jaw ticked as the light turned from red to green and he pulled out into traffic.

"I should have been there for him. If I wasn't cooking with you…"

"You're blaming me for Mason hurting himself?" He shook his head, rubbing the back of his neck with one hand.

"No. I…"

He pulled into the hospital parking lot, letting the car idle at the entrance. "You are. You're blaming me, us, this." Gripping the steering wheel with both hands, he wouldn't look at her. "You're serious right now?"

She opened her mouth but no words came out. She wasn't blaming *him* for Mason getting hurt, not exactly anyway, but she *was* blaming their relationship on…something.

"We should just call time before we go any further and our lives get any more entwined," he said.

It hit her like a sucker punch to the gut. Before...what? They'd been in and out of each other's lives for as long as she could remember. They were already fucking entwined. He'd had his dick inside her, for Christ's sake, there wasn't much more entwining two people could do.

"Elliott, please...don't do this. Let's calm down and talk about it first." She stretched out to touch his forearm but he yanked it out of reach. "We're both worked up. We just need to ride the wave."

"No, Clare. You need to go be with your family." He pushed the unlock button on the inside of his door. "And since you're convinced I've destroyed your family and would make a sorry excuse for a stepfather, let's just end it now and be done with it, okay?"

He wouldn't look at her, he wouldn't let her touch him, and his words rattled around her ribcage leaving slashes on her heart. He wasn't wrong, not entirely. She needed to go be there for Mason, she didn't have time to deal with their collapsing relationship.

More than that, on some level she was holding him, *them* to task for the destruction of her home life. Maybe it would be best if they parted ways. Maybe there was a reason he'd left her all those years ago. Maybe there was a reason he was leaving her now.

Maybe they just weren't meant to be together.

Without a word, she slid from the car and closed the door with a soft thud. She had no real idea how she found herself standing watching the taillights on the back of Elliott Swift's car as he pulled out of the hospital and drove away. But she knew one thing—it tore her up every bit as much as it had done when they were teenagers. More so, even.

Eventually, she pulled herself from standing curb side and turned to walk into the hospital. Were they really over? Would he just need some time to calm down?

He'd been going through his own shit storm too, that had to be contributing to his emotions, but were they really done?

Her phone rang with another voicemail as she made her way into the hospital. It was her boss telling her that the candidate who had been selected for the manager's position at the office couldn't accept it, and since she'd placed second in the process, he was asking if she wanted it.

The man of her dreams had left her and driven away for the second time in her life, and she was finally being offered the job she'd wanted for years but couldn't take.

The universe sure had a fucked up way of taking care of business.

"Where the fuck have you been?" The Sperm Donor grabbed her arm and dragged her around the corner out of earshot of Mason's room.

His fingers bit into her skin. Wrenching her arm, she tried to break free from his hold, but couldn't. "You're hurting me," she ground out through clenched teeth. "Let me go before I start screaming."

When he let her go, she rubbed at her arm. "I didn't have cell service. I came as soon as I got your messages. How is he?"

He folded his arms and his scowl deepened. "You really think that's it? That I'm just going to ignore the fact you dropped the ball once again on your maternal duties to our son just to go get your jollies off? Seriously, Clare?"

She held up a hand. "Mason. How is he?"

"You're fucking lucky I'm letting you even see him."

She tried again. "Does he need surgery?"

He shook his head. "They're keeping him overnight. They're going to take a look again in the morning once the swelling has gone down a bit. The scans weren't really conclusive one way or the other."

She nodded, ignoring his loud intake of air like he was

gearing up to berate her all over again, and strode into Mason's room.

Her vibrant and outgoing kid looked so small and pale in the middle of the big hospital bed and Catriona napped on the couch facing the bed.

"Hey kiddo."

"Hey, Mom. Did you learn how to make that chocolate thing?"

She smiled. "I did. I'll make it for you next time you visit, just like I promised. I'm sorry I wasn't here sooner. I had no cell service."

"I knew you'd come as soon as you could. You always do."

His words did little to ease the heavy weight sitting on her chest. She sat on the edge of his bed and picked up his good hand as tears coursed down her face. "I'm so sorry, baby. I shouldn't have gone somewhere that I didn't have service."

A frown pinched his tiny features. "Did you know you couldn't get calls when you went there?"

She shook her head and sniffed.

"Then why are you upset at yourself?"

Things were so simple for kids, so straightforward—gray areas just didn't exist. To Mason it was as simple as she didn't know. To her, guilt consumed her every cell making it hard to breathe or think clearly.

He yawned. "They gave me something that made me sleepy. Will you stay?"

"Try to stop me."

A nurse came in to check his blood pressure, pulse, and make sure he was comfortable. "You must be Mason's mom. I'm Betty, I'm going to be his nurse overnight."

She nodded, unable to stop her tears and sniffling.

Betty patted her shoulder. "He's just fine, Mama. Just fine. He's in the best place he could be. We're taking very good care of him. That couch pulls out into a bed—can't say it's overly comfy, but it means you'll at least be close by if you want to be."

"I'm the one that'll be staying." The Sperm Donor's hard voice filled the room, and Cat started awake.

"I want Mom to stay, Dad. You can go home. I'll see you tomorrow." Mason spoke without even opening his eyes and gripped her hand tighter.

Cat sat up and stretched. "I'll get an Uber home and come back tomorrow after school if you're still here, okay, squirt?" She ruffled his hair before leaning over to drop a kiss on his head. Rare moments when they weren't sniping at each other or arguing were Clare's favorite and her heart warmed at the affection between them.

"I'd rather you didn't Uber at this time of night by yourself, Cat." Clare gave her The Mom Look.

"It's not that late, and I'll be Ubering by myself at college in a few months. Relax, it's not my first Uber. And you have that friend finder thing on your phone. We both know I'm too chatty to be kidnapped. They'd want to return me in a matter of minutes."

Clare couldn't even find the energy to laugh.

"I'm done here. I'll bring you some bedding and a cup of tea if you'd like?" Betty's warm smile made her feel better.

"Thank you, Betty. I appreciate it."

The Sperm Donor kissed Mason goodbye, threw a glare in Clare's direction, and skulked out of the room.

"My Uber is around the corner, I'm going to head out, too." Cat gave Mason another kiss and squeezed Clare so hard she thought her eyes might pop out of her skull. "Love you, Mom."

"Love you too, KitKat." She pinched her daughter's cheek like she wasn't a nineteen year old woman ready to step out into the world and make her mark.

Clare tossed and turned all night long on the lumpy pull-out bed. If she needed to stay another night at the hospital, she was going to go home and pick up her own damn pillow.

A second round of scans the following morning confirmed that Mason didn't need surgery—yet—they were going to cast his arm and see if it healed itself, rather than placing pins in his bones. She half expected him to ask to go home with her, but as she waved him and The Sperm Donor off, she summoned an Uber of her own and made her way back to her empty house.

Empty. Just like her heart.

She checked her phone for what had to be the billionth time. Still nothing from Elliott. Nothing. Not even a message to see how Mason was. Nada. Zip. Zilch. Rien. How the fuck could he just sit at home scratching his balls and not think to drop her a line to see how her kid was?

She grumbled as she emptied the dishwasher. She'd made it to lunch time without a nervous breakdown or calling him and demanding to know what the fuck his deal was. Her soup was reheating in the microwave, and she had thawed a bagel from Panera that she'd discovered in the back corner of her freezer.

The doorbell rang just as her soup pinged in the microwave. What the fuck was the deal with the timing of the cosmos? Couldn't it just let one thing happen at a time? Her growling belly concurred.

Pulling the door open, her stomach dropped. She'd expected...hoped...prayed that Elliott would be standing in front of her with a bashful smile, ready to fix up what had broken between them, but instead, it was a mom from the ice rink. She hadn't spent much time with her, or any of the other moms for that matter, but her name definitely began with an N.

Natalie? Nora? Noelle? What the hell was the woman's name?

"Nova." She peeked out from around a huge basket in her hands. "It's Nova."

"Huh?"

"My name. It's Nova. You were muttering 'N' names to yourself and I figured I'd help a girl out."

"Oh God. I wasn't."

She nodded, pushing her way into the house past Clare. "You were. Sorry. Rude, I know. But this is heavy as fuck and I need to put it down somewhere. Kitchen?"

Clare pointed. "Through there."

Nova shuffled the gift basket through the house and placed it with care onto the breakfast bar. "I know our kids don't play for the same team." She braced her hands against the back of her hips and stretched out the curve of her spine. "But we heard about Mason's accident, and I wanted to stop by and see how he's doing."

She glanced over her shoulder, then back to Clare.

"He's at his Dad's." The words ripped through her chest. Her lip quivered and she blinked four hundred times in quick succession to fight the welling tears already spilling down her cheeks.

"Oh, honey. Come here." Nova enveloped her in such a tight hug that it felt like she might not fall apart for a whole thirty seconds. "Do you have wine? Something stronger?" Nova pushed her back by the biceps before plopping her onto a chair at the dining table and making herself at home around the kitchen.

Opening the microwave she breathed in deep. "Holy shitballs this soup smells delish."

She couldn't help but crack a smile.

"You want me to bring it over?"

Clare nodded and let the near stranger wait on her. Nova pulled the container from the microwave and ladled the soup into the bowl Clare had placed on the counter.

"There's enough for two, if you want some."

"I was going to ask, but I was trying to be polite. I'm starving, and I'm drooling right now at the smell of this. You made this from scratch?" She pointed a spoon at the bowl she was handing to Clare.

Another nod. She had no idea what was happening, but something in her gut said to just roll with Hurricane Nova and see where things went.

When she sat down with her own bowl of soup, Nova peered around the gift basket in the middle of the table. "I shoulda put this on the floor, right?" She eased it onto the tiles and focused her attention back to Clare.

"Wanna talk about it?"

Did she? She had no idea. What could she say other than she'd fucked everything up and felt more alone than she ever had before in her whole entire life? Fuck she was pathetic.

Nova blew on a spoonful of soup before sipping it. "Holy. Fuck. I need this recipe. It's so good. Wild rice, right? And veggies? I bet it's healthy. I need healthy." She patted her nonexistent tummy.

"My kid moved out to live with his dad and I feel like a momumental fuck up." She dropped her spoon before she'd even taken a bite. "I mean monumental."

"No, mom-u-mental is a pretty good description for the level of mom-guilt we suffer through."

She wasn't wrong.

"What else you got?"

"I think I ruined everything with Elliott. Cat is moving out soon, and I'm in denial about that. I want to stick a chastity belt on her, wrap her in bubble wrap and never let her leave the house again."

At that, Nova laughed. "I feel that on a deep and spiritual level." She took another mouthful of soup. "But I'm told society frowns on that kind of thing. Can't imagine why."

"I bust my ass every damn day, and I just..." She burst into a flood of tears before covering her face with her hands. "I'm sorry. I don't even know you. I'm just..."

"Overwhelmed? Lonely? Freaking out?"

"All of the above."

"Let me guess. You're blaming your relationship with dishy Coach Swift for everything falling down around your ears at home."

Clare jerked her head up. "He told you?"

Nova waved her hand. "God, no. I'm sure he's not the gossiping type. But I've been there. I'm a single mama who has kissed more than her fair share of frogs. You wouldn't believe the amount of shit I've tried to blame on my boyfriends."

"Like what?" Clare dragged her spoon through her soup and watched the rice swirl in its wake.

"Eat the soup before I lick my bowl clean then take yours and clear your bowl, too."

She smiled and reluctantly took a bite.

When Nova seemed satisfied that Clare had eaten enough, she continued. "I blamed them for everything. Fights with my kid—newsflash, parents fight with their kids. All the damned time. It's part of the job requirement." She blew on a spoonful of soup before shoveling it into her mouth. "There's a reason 'no' is one of the first words a child learns to say."

"What's that?"

"To torment us, I guess? I blamed them for my piling up laundry, for shit going to hell at work... You name it, I found a guy to blame it on.

"My point is, Cat isn't growing up and moving out because of Elliott. Mason didn't leave here to move in with his dad because of your relationship with Elliott. Or whatever else you're blaming him for, for that matter."

She picked up her bowl and carried it to the sink, holding it under the running water. "New relationships bring new challenges, for everyone. But they often aren't the cause of all the world's problems."

Was Nova right? Had Elliott been an easy scapegoat to blame for pulling her attention away? Perhaps, but given their history, her fear of him leaving—yet again—well, he'd kind of gone and done everything she'd feared he would.

"Maybe the kid will see that the grass isn't always greener and come back, you don't know that. Kids will be kids. Hell, if my kid thought he could come here and live in Mason's room for a while I'm sure he'd jump at the chance right off the bat. But it wouldn't take him too long to realize that you have rules just like his own mom does."

Clare's phone buzzed on the table in front of her: work again. She'd told her outgoing boss she'd give them an answer on the promotion in a few days. Her gut still said no, but her heart held her back from cutting that cord just yet.

Silencing her phone she took another mouthful of soup— perhaps if she kept filling her mouth she wouldn't have to say any of the self-loathing things fizzing at the back of her mind.

People wouldn't leave her if she wasn't awful, it was just that simple. If Elliott couldn't handle her, her life, maybe it really was best for them not to be together.

That sent a pang into her chest which she rubbed aggressively. Ugh.

If he wasn't meant to be with her, why the hell did it all feel so wrong each time he left?

CHAPTER 18
Elliott

"Elliott Swift would you stop your sulking and get your ass up off that couch before you start leaving butt prints in my sofa cushions?"

"Colorful, Dad. Real nice." Elliott still stood though, the last thing he needed was for his aging father to throw his slipper at him—those suckers hurt.

With a stretch up tall, and another to touch his toes, he shook himself out. Dad was right. Elliott had been hiding out in his living room for days. Fuck, had it been weeks? It couldn't have been weeks.

Every day had been the same since he'd dropped Clare off at the hospital. Time didn't matter, food didn't matter... He sniffed. Huh, turned out personal hygiene didn't matter either.

He scratched his chin. A five o'clock shadow was long behind him and it wasn't even playoff time. For the past... however long he'd been avoiding the world...he'd done the bare minimum: gotten up at 5AM, gone for a run, shower and a protein shake, then hockey practice, hockey practice, hockey practice. Sometimes he'd spice it up with a trip to the store for more protein powder, a smattering of hockey games, and collapsing into bed.

It was kind of pathetic. He hadn't broken his silence and messaged Clare, but Cat had told Theo who'd told him that Mason was going to be just fine, a cast for a few weeks and he'd be back on the ice in no time.

The more interesting thing was why Cat was even talking to Theo. Why hadn't she just told Elliott directly? Unless she didn't know that things had gone pear-shaped between him and her mom...

"Stop frowning, you'll get even more wrinkles." Dad stood at the stove, heating a pot of water with an egg in it.

"Dad, what are you doing? Let me help."

Dad thwapped his hand with the silicone spatula. "I might be old and losing it, but I'm not an idiot. I can boil a goddamn egg."

The sad truth was, he couldn't.

"I've been thinking..."

"Did it hurt, old man?" Despite his exhaustion, Elliot did his best to keep both their spirits up. They'd been to see Mom earlier in the day, and she had seemed to be doing a little better, too.

Another smack with the spatula. "As a matter of fact, it did. I think I'm ready to join your mom in that assisted living place, whatever it's called...the old people's prison." He brandished the kitchen tool once again. "But you'd better come visit."

He chuckled. "Like they could keep me away."

"I saw some flyers on the bulletin board this morning, when we were there. They have a chess club. I haven't played chess in years, used to be a state champ though, so that could be fun. Cribbage—apparently that's still a thing. And I think I'll bring in a deck of Uno cards and start an Uno championship." He grinned. "Those oldies don't stand a chance against me and my Uno deck."

It was such a 180 from his previous stance that Elliott hardly dared believe it. Was he testing the water? Was he waiting for Elliott to say "no, it's okay, please don't go"?

"It's time, son. You need to get out of your shitty apartment. When I move out you can put this place on the market, buy somewhere closer to work, and start putting yourself first for a change."

"Dad..." Elliott stepped around him to get a plate from the cupboard. "You don't need to move just for me."

Dad shook his head. "I'm not. I'm moving for me. And your mom. Maybe if I was in the same building she'd fight a little harder, or longer." His lip quivered. "And if she doesn't, then I'll have people around me and I won't feel like such a lonely old coot holding back his grown son. I'll take whatever extra time I can get with her."

No amount of swallowing could clear the lump in the back of his throat. "Dad..." His voice broke, but he tried again. "You're not holding me back."

Dad patted his hand. "You have to stop using us as a crutch and figure your shit out."

Wow. Don't hold back, old man.

"I know you've probably been thinking about moving back here, even though it's too far from the university. It's madness, Elliott. I won't let you do it. I can still live a good life in one of those places, and I can see more of your mother. It'll do me fine. It's time, son."

He *had* been contemplating moving across town and accepting the ball-busting stop-and-go traffic along the commute, but he hadn't been able to bring himself to bite the bullet and commit.

Dad moving into assisted living suddenly felt like an

unnecessary sacrifice. Elliott was a grown man. He should be able to help out his own fucking father, right?

He sighed. At the end of the day Dad needed more help around the house than he could give him, and he'd point-blank refused accepting someone else in the house to help him out. This was the best outcome.

So why didn't it feel like it?

He'd lived for almost forty years and had nothing to show for it but a failed marriage and a handful of dusty old hockey trophies in his parent's garage. It was kind of pathetic. When he was with Clare she didn't make him feel like a washed up has-been, she made him feel like he still had so much to give.

His stomach had hurt ever since he pulled away from her, standing with her arms wrapped across her body, outside the hospital. He'd thought they were making progress, mending fences, moving forward, together.

He hadn't planned on ever leaving her again, and while he knew he wasn't the father of her children, he had intended on being a damned good friend and role model to both of them while he loved their mother. A tiny voice in the back of his head dared dream that maybe they'd even try for a little one of their own someday.

Did she really blame him for the shit going on at home?

"What about that ex-wife of yours?" Dad brought him out of his misery with a jolt with different misery. He scooped the egg from the boiling water with a slotted spoon and shuffled across the kitchen to the toaster.

Elliott switched off the stove and dumped the pot of water in the sink.

"She's still ignoring letters from my lawyer." He sighed and rubbed his neck. "I don't know why she's being so difficult. It's not like she wants me back."

King-of-the-side-eye Dad, narrowed his gaze. "And what about Clare. You'd been seeing a lot of her there for a while and these past weeks..." He snapped his fingers. "Not a whisper. Did you fuck it up again?"

Good ole Dad, telling him how it was. Had he fucked it up again? Had he bailed too fast? Should he have stood his ground, planted his feet, and told her he wasn't going anywhere?

Yes. On all fucking counts, yes.

It had only been a couple weeks, but the pain of not seeing her smile, not hearing her laugh, or make him the butt of her jokes had left a black hole festering in his chest.

"She—"

"That woman has had a rough go of things, son. And I know we should have told you about it at the time, but your mom and me... We didn't want you getting stuck here, especially for a kid that wasn't your own." He rolled the egg on the counter to soften the shell. "We wanted you to go and follow your dreams, to chase the big scary stuff."

He picked at the shell, tossing it into the trash as he plucked pieces from the egg. "That said, you still found your way back to each other after all this time. Maybe you're supposed to be together." He shrugged like he wasn't commenting on the biggest relationship of Elliott's entire life. "Maybe we shouldn't have stood between you."

There was no point in getting into an argument with him over something they could no longer change. As much as Elliott didn't agree with his parents' decision to keep the truth about Clare from him, he understood it. It came from a place of love to protect him from himself.

"Why do you think it was something I did?"

For a long moment all Dad did in response was raise an eyebrow. "You're standing here moping in my kitchen aren't you?"

The man had a point. Kind of. But she'd as much as told him if he'd left again he'd better stay gone. And he had. He'd stupidly left her standing at the side of the road. He'd ruined everything. Again.

He smashed his egg onto a slice of toast. "Whatever you did, I'm sure you can fix it, as long as you fight for her. She might not forgive you again if you don't."

He wasn't sure she'd forgiven him for leaving her the first time, never mind abandoning her at the hospital when her kid was hurt, and not checking in with her since. So, yeah, okay, he had shit going on in his life, and yeah, okay, she was stressed out and had shit going on in hers, but at the end of the day, it really was him who had left her, once again.

Jesus Christ.

Maybe if he'd listened to what she had to say instead of knee jerking and pushing her away, he wouldn't have spent the past while missing her so damn much. It wasn't so much a miscommunication as it was him just being a dumbass.

But if she hadn't even forgiven him for the first time, what could he do to convince her that he wasn't going to leave her again when it was all he seemed capable of doing?

"Coach?"

Elliott lifted his head from his hands and met Linc's concerned eyes and furrowed brow. "What can I do for you, Lincoln?"

"I came here to ask you the same thing, Coach."

Elliott jerked his head back, and Linc pushed himself away from the doorframe and stepped inside his office. As he closed the door behind him, Elliott stretched out his leg, pushing the chair in front of his desk closer to Linc. "Take a seat."

Linc dropped onto it with a sigh. "You killed us out there this morning, Coach." He rubbed his thigh. "Kenzie is gonna have to work overtime to get all these knots out."

Elliott chuckled. He *had* pushed them hard during practice. Whether he was punishing them, or himself, he wasn't really sure. "You can take it."

Linc's nod was slow and something in his eyes suggested he wasn't sitting in Coach's office to talk about how exhausted he was. He had never been one to complain about some hard work.

"What's going on, Linc?"

The kid scratched the back of his head, but to his credit, he never broke eye contact. "I know you won't want to hear it, Coach. But we're worried about you."

Tension ratcheted up a notch in Elliott's heavy shoulders despite warmth spreading in his chest at his team captain's obvious concern. "You're right, I don't want to hear it." Partly because they were well within their right to be concerned about him, and partly because the thought of his team gossiping about him made him queasy.

He sighed, urging his shoulders to leave his ear-space and go back to where they were supposed to be. "But I told you the day I handed you that 'C' that I'd always listen to what you had to say. Always. Even when I don't like it."

Linc nodded again. "That's why I'm here. You're distracted and pissed as hell, and while it hasn't cost us a game yet, it's come close a couple times these past few weeks."

Elliott stayed silent. The kid was right and he didn't want to gaslight him into believing he wasn't.

"Is it your parents? Did something happen to Coach Swift senior?"

Dad had coached Linc's ex-NHL superstar dad while he was in school. Elliott's team still called him Coach, too. It warmed his heart, and Dad always got a kick out of it when he used to stop by the rink for a visit or to watch practice.

He slid down his chair and tipped his head back. "No. Dad's okay. He moved into an assisted living facility this week.

We were pretty lucky they had a spot in the same place as Mom, but they're both there now. It's a weight off."

A pang of guilt struck him as he winced. "I didn't mean..." Raking a hand over his face he shook his head. He shouldn't feel so relieved that Dad was somewhere he was less likely to hurt himself, versus being somewhere with Elliott taking care of him instead, but he did. The relief was like aloe on sunburn, instant and damn near overwhelming.

"It's okay. I get it. When Dad convinced Gramps to go into a nursing home I saw such a change in him. In both of them. Dad wasn't feeling stressed out every day that Gramps might set the house on fire or wander down the street naked." Linc leaned forward, the corner of his mouth twitching. "That happened twice before Gramps agreed it was time and something needed to give."

Blowing out a long, slow breath, Elliott rubbed the bridge of his nose. "I have to clear out and sell their house, which is, y'know, a lot since it's my childhood home and all. But it's too far from school to move there."

Why the fuck was he unpacking this shit to one of his players? He wasn't his guidance counsellor—hell, he wasn't even his friend. If anyone should be unloading to anyone, it should have been Linc to Elliott.

"Anyway. My parents are fine."

Linc pursed his lips. "Good. That's good. So your troubles are of a...female nature?" His cheeks pinked, and he winced as the words hung in the air between them.

Was he for real? He was really going there? In truth, Elliott wasn't completely surprised. Linc was a mother hen on the team, and he had some of the biggest balls on the ice Elliott had ever seen. He also had no idea how fucking strong and capable he truly was.

"I can figure it out by myself, Linc. But I appreciate you

coming in here to talk. But while I have you here... You wanna tell me what's going on with you and Enzo?"

Linc flexed his jaw. "Not really."

"You two gonna be able to work it out?"

A defiant jerk of Linc's chin made the light bounce off the whirlpool of emotions swirling in the boy's eyes. "I will if he keeps his hands off my fucking sister."

Ah. Woman troubles of a different nature.

"You'd think after Finn and Will he'd learn not to fuck around..." Linc shuddered. "I can't even. Dude wants to date my sister. I told him to fuck all the way off." He steadied himself with a slow breath. "Nice try, Coach. But I'm not here to put my brother on blast. He knows how I feel about it, and we're moving forward. This..." He pointed his finger back and forth across the space between them. "This is about you."

"I'm good, thanks."

Linc didn't move. Instead, he held his gaze, there was no judgment or amusement in his stare, only concern. Maybe he *should* open up to the kid, maybe it would somehow help them *both* if Elliott could figure out how the fuck to get out of the quagmire he'd fallen into with Clare.

"I fucked things up with Clare. Again. And I have no idea how to fix it."

Linc's solemn nod bordered on hilarious. "It's cool, Coach. We all make mistakes. And I can tell you from personal experience, us Snow Pirates sure know how to fuck things up on a monumental scale."

He couldn't help but laugh at Linc's bluntness. He wasn't wrong. And being included as part of the Snow Pirates family of fucked-up-ness tickled his heart.

But if Elliott knew anything about anything, he knew that not only did the Snow Pirates know how to mess things up, they also knew how to fix it. They were becoming somewhat famous for their grand gestures to win back their partners.

Hell, they'd just thrown a freakin' prom because Morrison had royally screwed things up with his girl.

It ain't nothin' but a family thing.

He wasn't sure he could pull off something so grand, nor was he sure it was even something that would work for Clare, but if it's what the guys thought he should do, he'd try anything. He needed to get her back. He needed her to believe he was staying forever. He needed her to trust him.

He had no idea how to repair fractured trust other than time, but if she wouldn't talk to him, if she was truly done... A shiver passed through him. It didn't bear thinking about.

Mason was going to be a Snow Pirate someday. He'd see him—both of them—at practices and games and if she wasn't his, he wasn't sure he could even stand it.

His stomach twisted. It couldn't be over between them. The universe had conspired to bring them back together after all those years apart. This was their time. It had to be.

"We can help you fix it, Coach. We just need to figure out your big 'I'm sorry I fucked up, please forgive me' moment."

He snickered. "Like I didn't know that. I have no idea what to do to show her I love her, that I'm invested in our relationship, and I never want to leave her again. She's always so busy, it's not like I can give her the gift of time or anything."

And he had done exactly what she'd been afraid of him doing and left her. She probably thought he was stewing in stubbornness, when in fact he just had no idea how to make it right in a way she deserved.

Linc smiled. "Yeah, time turners don't really exist. So that's out..."

Raking a hand through his hair, Elliott slunk lower in his seat. Perhaps just talking at Linc would prompt some kind of brilliant way to fix things. "She's lonely. Mason moved in with his dad, Cat is leaving for college, the house is falling down around her ears. She doesn't go out much. I mean, I could probably fill her freezer with ice cream, but I don't think that's what we're going for."

He bolted upright. "Wait. What if I take care of some of the things around her house that need fixing? The kitchen faucet is leaky, and there are floor tiles stacked next to her kitchen door that need laying. The fence in her yard needs to be painted. A storm took out part of the decking in her backyard a million years ago and she hasn't fixed that yet either."

He tapped his chin, not waiting for an answer. "She mentioned she'd love to sit outside more, but when she does she just gets pissed at the list of things that needs to get fixed that she doesn't have time for. What if I fix it all for her?"

Again, not waiting for Linc to chime in with an opinion, he kept going. "I mean, I don't know that I could find a way to get her out of the house long enough to do it all by myself, but I could try, right? I could make a start and just do a bit at a time. I could mow the lawn, put down mulch, see if she's killed every plant in the garden or if there's a chance for any of them."

"I mean, it doesn't say I love you forever and want to be with you, but it would make her life a bit more comfortable for her, right? And if I just keep showing up in her space and refusing to leave, that'll show her I'm sticking around, right?"

"Do you want me to answer any of these questions? Or do you just want to keep riffing until you come to a decision? I'm really not sure. Not for nothing though,"—Linc picked up a pen from the desk and pointed it at him—"that last one sounds dangerously close to stalking, Coach. That's illegal."

"Does it sound like something? I can't say I'm known for my ability to fix my fuck-ups. And we know from my divorce history that I don't know shit about women. You're probably more experienced in that area than I am."

Linc laughed. "I had it easy with Cleo compared to some of the guys. But I think even if Clare never wants to see you again, making her life a little easier as a single mom is a noble goal all the same. You know, we could probably help you with that. If you'd let us anyway."

"Help me, how?"

"Oh, I dunno. It's not like you have a bunch of strapping young men who are competent enough to wield a paintbrush or anything." He scratched his chin. "Some of us could probably even handle a wrench or a saw."

Elliott held up a hand. "One thing at a time. I'm not sure I'm ready to hand some of the guys a paintbrush, never mind anything more dangerous."

"That's fair. But think about it, Coach. Many hands make light work and all that jazz, isn't that what you always say? You've had our backs for years—let us have yours for a change. Let us help you get the girl back."

Linc's smile and hopeful tone were infectious. Elliott was less than convinced it would be enough to win Clare back, but with any luck it would be enough to open the door to peace talks. And with even more luck, he'd find a way to convince her he wasn't going to leave her ever again.

He'd always thought of himself as an unlucky person, but the universe had brought her into his life twice—didn't that make him the luckiest man in the world?

CHAPTER 19
Clare

Clare was half a pint of cookie dough ice cream, a share size bag of sour cream Lays, and three retro chick flicks deep. She'd watched *Sleepless in Seattle*, *My Best Friend's Wedding*, *Pretty Woman*, and *Runaway Bride*. Clearly she'd been feeling a strong Julia Roberts vibe for the evening. She didn't disappoint, either. Neither did Meg.

Clare mouthed along to almost every single word of *Pretty Woman*—her absolute favorite. And when Vivian—aka Julia—said *"the bad stuff is easier to believe,"* Clare broke down into her ice cream. Why was it that the bad stuff about yourself was always easier to believe than the good?

Why was it that it took years of hard work to accept positive things about yourself, and a fraction of a second to believe the negative?

Why was it that the negative shit stayed with you for your entire life and the positive rolled off you as quickly as it had been said?

She stabbed at the ice cream with her spoon, no longer hungry and instead, verging on nauseous. What kind of asshole just disappeared—not for the first fucking time either —for weeks on end because shit got hard?

Wasn't shit *always* hard? Wasn't that just being a fucking grown up?

Her fucking asshole. That's who.

Her stomach churned, the creamy dessert roiling around in her gut like it was a damned ice cream maker. She'd fallen for him even harder the second time, and yet, the outcome was still the same as the first.

Stab. Stab. Stab. Jabbing the spoon into the ice cream wasn't at all necessary, but it sure helped channel some of her rage. Stab. Stab.

The front door burst open and Mason trudged into the house, pulling his suitcase behind him. "I'm back."

That was all she got. The Sperm Donor was nowhere to be seen, and Mason slammed the door shut before dumping his case at the bottom of the stairs and bolting up to his room.

That was it? He was back? Back, back? Or do my laundry so I can leave again, back?

"Mase-Mallow? Is everything okay?" Her stomach fluttered as she called up the stairs after him.

"Don't make it a thing, Mom. I'm back."

"I'm not. I mean... I'm glad you're back, of course I am. But I just want to make sure you're okay."

"I'm fine, Mom. My case is full of dirty clothes, though, sorry."

She chuckled. "I can handle that. But get your ass down here and put those dirty clothes in the laundry room, please."

"But Moooooooom!"

Catriona skipped down the stairs. She'd been so quiet all evening that Clare had forgotten she was even home.

"You've been awfully quiet this evening. What are you up to? Do you have a boy hiding in your room?"

Cat snorted. "Other than listening to you sob to all those super old movies? You'll see."

Not just old movies, but super old movies. Ouch. If she was honest with herself the movies had been considered "old" when she was in college, so they must be—gulp—classics now. Antiques? Shit. Fuck. She was basically a fossil. A single-as-a-Pringle fossil. She should just be put out to pasture already.

"Can you come here a sec?" Cat jerked her head toward the stairs.

"Where are we going?"

"Just to the office. Mase-Monster and I need to talk to you about something real quick."

Oh god. Talk to her about what? Fuck. Was he only back temporarily? Was he leaving again? Was Cat ready to move out already? Where was this going?

On the left wall in Clare's office, Catriona had tacked family pictures from over the years. Clare ran a finger over the shiny photos as a wave of nostalgia crashed into her. "What's all this?"

"Mom." Cat planted her hands on her hips. "You've put Mason and me first for our whole lives—and then some. Since you got pregnant with me. You never put yourself first."

Mason pushed past Clare to get to Cat and stood mirroring his big sister, hands on both hips. Despite their obvious differences, the family resemblance was still there. They were definitely both her kids.

"It's time to put yourself first for a change." Cat's scowl was again mirrored by Mason's.

"We think you need to start doing things for you, things you love. We see you working so hard all the time, in a job you're not truly happy in even though you pretend to be. And we think it's time for you to spread your wings, like you're always telling us to."

Clare's jaw dropped open. Were her two teenage kids really

using her own words against her? Dammit why did she have such smart and quick offspring? Couldn't they just pretend to listen to her sermons like other kids did with their parents?

"I—"

Cat waved an open hand. "Whatever excuse you're about to come up with, we don't want to hear it. We're both getting older. I'm leaving for school, and Mason is back home now, but you still need to start living too. For yourself, not for us."

Tears welled in Clare's eyes at her daughter's heartfelt words.

"I know you're thinking of turning down that promotion they offered you at work, but I really think you should take it, Mom. I think you should start chasing your dreams with as much passion and determination as you encourage us to chase ours."

Fuck. When had Catriona gotten so fucking eloquent? That certainly hadn't come from Clare. What an amazing woman she was raising. But was she also right? Wasn't it her job as their mother to always put them first?

Wasn't it her job to keep her hopes and dreams on hold until she'd helped them reach theirs? Had she been wrong this whole time to keep her own passions at bay?

Mason's tongue poked out the side of his mouth as he jammed his finger into his cast. "Agh. So itchy."

Clare stepped between the kids to her desk and opened the middle drawer. When she produced a metal ruler, his face lit up. "Don't make it weird, Mom. We're worried about you. We want you to be happy. And you're not. You're always so busy. And when you're not busy with work, you're busy taking care of us. You need to chill out a bit more."

"Or, y'know, any." Cat's mumbled addition was still loud enough to be heard and her cheeks pinked as Clare's brow arched in response.

That was her freakin' job as a mother. And if she took the

new role at work she would very likely end up even busier. There just weren't enough hours in the fucking day. But their words did give her pause.

"You should take the job, Mom. You earned it. And even if things get even more hectic, well, I'll come home for weekends, and Mason will help out more around the house."

Mason snorted and waved his cast. "I'm decrepit."

"I don't think that's the word you're looking for Mase." Cat ruffled his hair, and Clare's heart almost imploded. The older they got the closer they grew. As much as she—sometimes—missed the days of their teasing and chasing each other around the house, this...this was so much nicer.

"You always tell us that we gotta try. If we don't try, we'll never know. If you don't take the new job and give it a try, you'll never know if it's what you always dreamed of."

She wasn't sure she'd ever seen Mason look quite so smug. She hated when they turned her words back against her, but they also really did have a point. Even if she hated the new role, she would know and could work toward something else in its place, instead of always wondering what if.

"Are you going to take it?" Cat's hard, level gaze was one Clare herself had practiced for decades. It was one of determination and so full of confidence and inherent belief that Clare couldn't bring herself to say no.

But she also made a point of never lying to her kids. As she stood next to them, she stared at the pictures on the wall—Catriona's first steps, Mason's first goal in hockey, family picnic in the park when they got soaked in the rain. Tracing her fingers over snapshots from over the years, she couldn't think of anything she wanted to do more than make her kids proud of her.

Her fingers stopped on a worn, creased piece of pink paper next to a picture of Clare's first ever picture holding Cat in her arms. "Where did you get this?"

"You left it on the dining table. I almost threw it out. It looked so old and out of place. I'm glad I opened it."

It was the letter she'd written to herself that Elliott had given her over lunch that day he stopped by. The last line of the letter said: *Do the scary things, Clare. You can do it all.*

She had always been a lead-by-example kind of person, and she was going to lead by motherfucking example and do the hard and scary thing.

Catriona arched a brow. "That's not an answer, Mom. Are you going to take it?" She planted her hands on her hips again and cocked her head as though she wouldn't take no for an answer.

Stomach flipping, Clare pulled her phone from her butt pocket and nodded. "I'll call him right now and tell him. I mean, he won't be working right now, but I'll leave him a message, okay?"

Both kids nodded, but didn't move.

"Frank, it's Clare. I'm just calling to let you know that I'd love to take the manager role if it's still available. Uh. That's it. Talk soon. Thanks." She hated leaving voicemails for her boss. One time, she'd gotten so flustered that she'd told him she loved him at the end of the message and she couldn't look him in the eye for two months.

Cat and Mason fist-bumped each other and hissed "yessss!"

"Do you feel better now?" Cat threw her arms around Clare.

"I feel a bit sick to be honest."

"Then let's open some wine." As Cat guided her back to the kitchen Mason followed behind. "Doesn't wine cure everything?"

Who could argue with that logic? "Not everything, but it's a start."

"Mom? Can we go to another Snow Pirates game?"

Mason's wide and hopeful eyes pleaded with her as they walked.

"Don't you want your dad to take you? That's always been your thing, kiddo."

She tossed a glance over her shoulder as she descended the stairs, and his little face was like he'd bitten into a slice of lemon. "It's cooler when you do it. He doesn't know people like you know people. Y'know?"

She did know. Her heart both swelled and shattered at the same time.

"Theo says he can take me skating again soon." The excitement in his voice was contagious, and she couldn't help but smile.

"That's great, Mase. And sure, let's get some tickets for another game, okay?"

"Tomorrow?"

She wasn't ready to see Elliott quite so soon, but the hope in Mason's voice forced her to steady her nerves. When they got to the kitchen she turned to face him. "Please, Mom? I miss the smell of the ice." His gloomy face cracked her heart into another gazillion pieces.

"I know you do, kiddo." She paused for a minute and skimmed her finger down the page of the calendar on the fridge. "It looks like we're free tomorrow, so I can't see why not." Other than not wanting to lay eyes on the fucking coach of the team, anyway.

"Whoohoo!" He pumped both hands in the air and shook his booty.

"I'll take care of grabbing tickets."

His eyes lit up like she'd told him he could go hang out with TJ DeSantis—his favorite Wild player. "Thanks, Mom. You're so cool." Mason threw his arms around her waist and hugged so tight that for a minute she wasn't sure whether he'd let up or not. "Thanks for letting me come back, too."

Swallowing the lump in her throat she pulled him to her even tighter, curling her arms around him and squeezing. "You will never not be welcome here, Mason. No matter what. You hear me?"

He nodded against her torso. "I thought it'd be more fun living with Dad. But...it wasn't." He still hadn't let go of her and his voice was muffled as he spoke. "I don't like her, Mom. She's not a nice person."

Her. The other woman. Oh, the things Clare could say. Biting her tongue, she patted his back. "That's okay, kiddo. We aren't always going to like everyone we meet."

"I thought I'd like her more if I spent more time with her. But that's not what happened. I like her even less now. My plan totally backfired and bit me in the ass."

Squashing down the laugh bubbling up in her chest and fighting the urge to break into dance at the fact Mason agreed with her, she pulled him back from her and made him look up at her. "That's okay, Mase. You tried, right? Now you know. If you want to keep your distance from her, that's okay too. And if you need help talking to your dad about setting some boundaries, I can totally help you with that, too."

"Do you think Dad will be mad at me?"

She didn't hesitate before answering. "Hell, no. Absolutely not."

In all honesty, he probably would be, but she wasn't going to let him. It wasn't Mason's fault The Sperm Donor picked a sour-faced bitch to cheat on her with.

"I'm sure he's grateful that you gave her a really good shot before making your decision. And your opinion of her may change as you grow older. Just because you don't like her now, doesn't mean you'll dislike her forever." Wow. How had such calm civility come spewing out of her mouth when her insides sizzled like they'd been drenched in acid?

In reality, Clare would dislike both The Sperm Donor *and*

his bit on the side forever—and then some. She sure knew how to hold a grudge.

"Mom?" Mason's small voice made something in her chest twinge.

"Yeah, kiddo?"

"When are we seeing Coach Swift again? Do you think he'd sign my cast? Theo says he's going to get all the Snow Pirates to sign it for me. Can you believe it, Mom? All of them!"

The twinge in her chest grew to an all-out twist, and she cleared her throat. "I really don't know, Mase. He's pretty busy right now, y'know?" Her voice was charged with tension and sadness, but if he noticed, he didn't show it.

"Maybe we'll see him at the game, right?"

Her stomach clenched, and her heart sped up. She wasn't sure she could ever look at the man again without falling apart into a puddle of tears, but she had twenty-four hours to attempt to get her shit together before she had to find out.

"Yeah, kiddo. Maybe we'll see Coach Swift at the game."

Oh. Not only was Elliott fucking Swift *there*, but he saw her the minute she plonked her ass into her seat while cradling a giant foam finger with one hand and a bucket of warm, buttered popcorn with the other.

She knew he saw her, could *feel* his eyes. She'd tried to get seats where he would be less inclined to notice her in the crowd, but it was as though he knew just where and when to look.

His eyes melted the plexi glass between them for the first two periods of the game. How he managed to coach the kids on the ice while spending so much time staring at her was anyone's guess.

In the third period, Clare couldn't sit still. She'd barely watched any of the damn game. For all she knew, giant clowns with banana skins as skates had taken over on the ice. If wishing made it so—then she might have a chance to escape from Elliott's piercing gaze.

She couldn't do it. She couldn't be held captive by his fucking eyes any longer.

It was as though a million ants were crawling over her skin. She needed to get out. Hockey games would remain the purview of Alex, and she'd never darken the door of the rink again. It was too much, too hard, too painful.

She might not know who was winning on the ice, but she could recall every detail about the man standing behind the players on the bench. His pale blue shirt, his more than a couple of day's growth covering his jaw, his tired eyes, his strained smile. She had committed it all to memory.

The invisible lines that had linked their hearts together since childhood grew taut and no amount of rubbing her chest or praying for the ache to stop made her feel better. Why couldn't he just show up for her when she needed him to? One fucking time—that's all she had asked for.

Why the hell did he run?

Always with the fucking running. Was she really that impossible to live with?

Self-loathing swirled in her brain. She couldn't spend her life questioning his motivations. She couldn't waste what little free time she had aching to be in his arms, to be the one he stepped up for, the one he fucking stayed for.

He either wanted her, or he didn't. And no amount of making eyes at her across the arena when he should have been paying attention to the game, changed the fact that when things had gotten even a little complicated, he'd fled—yet again.

The buzzer at the end of the third period had barely

sounded when she bounded to her feet, grabbed Mason by the arm, and hauled his reluctant ass from the arena.

He kept grumbling and asking why they couldn't hang out for a while to catch up with Elliott, but Clare just wanted to be as far away from him as possible. If he could run from things that made him uncomfortable, she could too. And she could only hope it fucking worked.

CHAPTER 20
Clare

"Monday, Monday." Clare pulled the car onto her street. Her bones ached and her left eye twitched. She was going to feed the beasts, then collapse into bed. Work had been a shit show, and she was already over Monday. All-the-way-over it.

"Ba-da ba-da-da-da." Cat and Mason sat together in the back seat, bobbing their heads as they joined in with her singing. They had far more vocal talent than she did, but she enjoyed the fact she was teaching them—as Mason called them—really old songs, and that they still entertained her after what felt like a long day at the office.

"So good to me."

A yawn surprised her as they rounded the final corner to the house interrupting her crooning. While it wasn't late by any means—she'd gotten away from the office just after lunch time as a rare treat and picked up groceries on her way—everything just felt like a little more work these days.

"Mom?" Mason shifted forward between the seats, his arm outstretched, finger pointing. "Whose cars are those by the house?"

She slapped at his arm. "Mason! Seatbelt! Sit back. We aren't in the driveway yet."

Three SUVs were parked at the curb in front of her house, not blocking her way into her garage, but still in her space. Maybe they were there visiting the neighbors?

A tall, dark, shirtless figure made his way across her front lawn and her heart sped up. The man—vaguely familiar, but she couldn't quite place him—had his arms full with a bag of what looked like leaves.

Who would strip half naked to steal leaves from someone's yard?

She reversed into the driveway, catching his eye as she threw the car into park and laughing as he struggled to shift the oversized bag enough to give her a smile and a wave. He definitely looked like he was supposed to be there, and the grubby marks over his cheeks and arms coupled with the sweat glistening on his way-too-young body suggested he had been there a while.

"Mom?" Mason asked, "Why is Russell Stewart in our yard hugging our leaves?"

Catriona's head snapped up from her phone. In the rear view, Clare made out the smallest of smiles teasing at her daughter's lips.

"Eyes forward, young lady. He's too old for you."

An eye roll, a sigh, and a flick of her hand followed. "I don't even like *that* one."

"*That* one." Clare's heart stopped dead in her chest. Those two words suggested that Cat liked a different "one," and Clare was *not* ready for her daughter to be involved with a jock.

She fanned herself, not quite knowing what the fuck was going on, and sucked in a shaky breath. As tempting as it was to stay in her car, she couldn't hide from whatever was happening in her yard forever. No matter how much she might have wanted to.

"All right, let's get out and figure out why the hell there's a half-naked Snow Pirate carrying yard waste to our trash cans." She eased out of the vehicle and shuffled to the trunk.

"Hey, Ms. Reynolds." Russell tossed the bag into the open trash can and gave her another wave. "Got groceries?"

She nodded, still not able to find her voice.

"I'll get 'em for you." He jerked his head. "You should head out back."

Would things make sense in the backyard? Or would her yard magically strip her of her shirt, too?

She might have been an old lady, damned near old enough to be Russell's momma, but the light kept catching his shiny, ripped chest, and it took everything to make herself stop staring.

As she approached the side gate to the yard, a hive of activity met her ears, chatting, laughter, the sound of a saw cutting through wood, and pop music playing from God only knew where.

She held out her hand across Mason's chest to stop him from going through the gate. She needed a second to compose herself. His brows pleated, so she held up two fingers, and forced another breath into her body.

Wait. What had happened to her creaky old gate? Her gate —or rather, her former gate—had been older than she was. It hung on one hinge and squeaked and scraped against the path as you fought it open.

A freshly painted gate hung at the entrance to her yard. She tugged it open and slipped through the space, hoping no one would notice her right away so she could get a lay of the land.

A shirtless Elliott leaned over a table with a circular saw, his sage green t-shirt tucked into the ass pocket of his jeans. A pencil jutted out from behind his ear as he worked a tape measure along a length of wood.

What seemed to be the entire Snow Pirates team—in various stages of undress—were working on her yard. Painting, mowing, weeding, doing everything she'd berated herself about not doing—for years.

What the fuck was he playing at? Her insides hardened, and she folded her arms in a bid to reinforce the protection from her ribs currently weakening around her heart as it swelled.

So he was doing some yard work, big fucking deal. Like that made up for everything he'd put her through?

The back door to the house swung open and Cat flitted down the stairs carrying a large tray laden with iced lemonade and Solo cups. Mason appeared behind her with a plate piled high with cookies.

Clare checked over her shoulder, wasn't he just right behind her? Were they in on it?

Traitorous crotch goblins.

She slid her thumbnail between her teeth and stayed silent, peeking around the edge of the house as her kids made their way around the yard offering drinks and snacks to the college kids doing manual labor.

Elliott stretched upright when Cat got to him, reaching his hands high and leaning to one side and Clare's mouth ran dry. He brushed his pinking forearm across his forehead and squinted in the sunshine. Good lord. He was dirty.

Flecks of dirt and blades of grass clung to his jeans, and like Russell, he had dirt on his cheeks. And he was sweaty. So deliciously sweaty.

She rolled her head back and said a silent prayer of thanks to every deity who was listening for an unusually warm April afternoon.

Heat pooled between her legs as he picked up a cup from Cat's tray and downed the lemonade in one go before getting a refill. Was everything in slow motion? She didn't care. Slow motion meant she got to watch him for even longer.

And fuck, did she ever watch.

She was about to fan herself with her hand, or the gate, when Cat pointed to her, and Elliott shifted so she was in his line of sight. He nodded and placed the cup back onto the tray before grabbing a rose from a glass of water on his work bench, clenching it between his teeth, and stalking toward her like some deliciously rugged animal and she was his prey.

When he got to her, he pulled the rose from his mouth and handed it to her. "There is no fire escape for me to climb like in the movie. I'd climb the fence"—he jerked his head toward the freshly painted fence to their side—"but it's still wet."

She took the rose, but her scowl stayed firmly in place. Re-enacting a scene from her favorite movie wasn't going to win her over after everything they'd been through, but she couldn't douse the flames in her heart at how sweet the moment was—even without the climbing.

"I know this doesn't make up for anything. It's...I guess it's all just a token. The yard, the rose..." He sniffed and wiped the side of his nose, his finger leaving a streak of sawdust on his face. "I couldn't just call and say I was sorry. It didn't feel like it would be nearly enough. Still doesn't."

She narrowed her eyes and crossed her arms again, taking care not to squish the rose, or scratch herself with the thorns.

"I'm sorry, CeeCee." His Adam's apple bobbed as he swallowed, and his eyes filled with tears. He reached for her, then hesitated when she didn't move to welcome his advance. "I shouldn't have dropped you at the hospital and ghosted you. I was butt hurt, my pride was wounded, and I guess all that shit with Denise just came rushing back, and I let my brain get the better of me. I couldn't figure out how to come back from that."

"Why didn't you call me, Eli? Mason got hurt." Her lip trembled, but she wouldn't cry. Goddammit, she would *not* cry.

He nodded. "I know. Cat kept me updated, but I know that's not the same thing as being there for him myself, for both of you. If I talked to you that would have meant things could have deteriorated even worse than they already were. Not that I can even imagine what that might look like. So I just..." He shrugged.

"I ran for real this time, I guess. Last time, sure, I went off to chase my hockey dream and when I got back I thought you were happy with someone else. But I came back. This time." He rubbed his stomach, bringing her attention back to his glistening chest and biceps.

"Fuck. I feel sick even talking about it. I just fled. I'm not proud of myself. And once I was out, I had no fucking clue how to come back without you telling me to go fuck myself. I thought somehow things would just magically work themselves out."

"Your dad slapped you upside the head and told you to figure your shit out, didn't he?" She still didn't crack her rock-solid wall of don't-fuck-with-me defense. But she also couldn't imagine Elliott having the wherewithal to just get his ass back into her space without a friendly nudge from his parents, which made her smile.

For a smart guy he could sometimes be a bit dense. He smiled back, warm, loving, and it damn near broke her heart. "I won't deny that Dad, and Linc, played a part in getting my ass back here to fix things—both in your yard and between us." He pointed a thumb over his shoulder toward the yard.

She couldn't see behind him, but she could feel the team's

eyes on them. The yard had grown quieter, the music had been turned down, and while the work continued, it was more than clear that Elliott's players were eavesdropping on their conversation.

"I don't do the feelings well. I'm a good provider, sure, you need something picked up at the store, or manual jobs done around the house, I'm your guy. But under stress... I bottle the feeling shit up tighter than a bottle of craft beer. I don't know what to do with it."

"It hurt that you left again, Elliott. And I don't know that I can trust you not to do it again." She turned the rose around in her fingers. "It's very nice of you to take it upon yourself to make my yard look pretty, but when it comes down to it... You left me, Eli."

Tears trickled down her cheeks, and she cursed herself as she swallowed, once, twice, a third time to try to get control of herself. "I'm so tired of everyone leaving me."

She'd barely finished her sentence before his arms were around her and she was squished against his sticky chest. He smelled of sweat and summer, but his arms held her together with such force it left her breathless.

"I know. I'm sorry. I really am. I know that nothing I say right now, or even do, will make it up to you. Nor will it do anything to make you believe I'm here to stay. But I am, CeeCee. I'm never letting you go again."

His grip around her tightened, and she softened against him. "I've been such a fucking idiot and I'm sorry. I let fear and my own inner monologue get in the way of what I wanted, and I hurt you in the process. I'm so sorry."

They stood wrapped in each other's arms for a couple more minutes. And while it wasn't a magic solution to their problem, it was a start. When he stepped back from her, his eyes still glistened.

"Three strikes and you're out." She clenched her jaw. "For good."

He nodded. "I don't deserve another shot, I know that. But if I ever leave again feel free to have the team beat me to death with their sticks."

She might just do that.

"Sorry. I'm a bit stinky." He offered her a cautious smile.

"You're not that bad. You look all rugged and shit though."

"Is it working for you?"

She took a step back and pinched her chin with her thumb and forefinger, assessing him with her gaze. "I mean..." She shrugged. "I guess so?"

"Well, if it's only working for you a little, I suppose I could put my shirt on. Y'know, stop offending those beautiful eyes of yours." He reached for his back pocket and she swatted his hand away.

"Don't. You. Fucking. Dare. You have a lot of making up to me to do for the past few weeks, and I think if you continued to parade around half naked it'd go some way to repairing things."

"That so?" His lips twitched.

She nodded.

"I really am so sorry, Clare. Hurting you is my least favorite thing to do." He brushed the curve of her cheek with his knuckles. "I can't promise it'll be the last time I hurt you. But I swear, it'll be the last time I ever leave."

Her heart clenched at his words as he closed the space between them and kissed her like they were the only people around. Her lips parted on a sigh while the team and presumably her kids, stood behind them clapping, hooting, and whistling at their PDA.

Okay, so everything wasn't instantly made better by a fresh coat of paint and some new decking, and only time would tell if Elliott truly meant what he'd said about never leaving her again. But the ache in her chest and the sourness in her gut that had lingered for the past few weeks had already started to dissipate. And the future certainly looked brighter than her recent past.

CHAPTER 21
Elliott

"I think this is the last of it." Elliott pushed through Clare's back door with his butt. When he made his way into the house, he spun to place the boxes of leftover pizza on the kitchen counter. "Theo grabbed the empties and dumped them in the trash."

Clare nodded. "Thanks. And Linc just brought a trash bag outside to collect all the paper plates and cups."

Ordering pizza for the team had been Mason's idea, no doubt in a not-so-subtle bid to keep his new best friends around just a little longer. They'd all taken a minute to sign his cast and snap selfies with him, and those who hadn't left in a hurry right after the pizza and beers were done, even played a little street hockey with him out in the street in front of Clare's house.

Clare hadn't loved the idea, what with his busted arm and all, but the boys went easy on him and Mason was still buzzing from the whole thing.

His face was flushed and his hair stuck out in all directions. "That was so freakin' cool."

"Come on, squirt. Let's go." Cat ruffled his hair and tossed a wink at Clare before grabbing the keys on her way through the kitchen.

"Catriona?"

Cat blew a kiss at her mom but didn't stop. "We'll be back later. Enjoy the peace and quiet." Her words were charged with knowing, and Clare's face turned the color of ripe strawberries.

When the front door clicked shut, Clare jumped into action. She grabbed the half full pizza boxes and put all of the leftover pizza into one box before shoving it on a shelf in the fridge. "I can feel you staring at me, Eli."

"Can't help it, CeeCee." He stepped up behind her and placed his hands over her hips, stilling her in front of him. Her body tensed for just a second, but by the time his lips grazed against the curve of her neck she'd relaxed against him with a sigh.

She reached her hand up and cupped his head while he nibbled his teeth along her shoulder. "You're so sexy, Clare." His dick hardened against the curve of her ass.

"Right. Super sexy." Her voice was breathless and she leaned her head even farther from him, giving him more access to her creamy skin. Pressing her ass against him, she reached back with both hands and pulled his hips against her. "Short shorts clearly do it for ya, eh, Coach?"

He nipped at her skin with his lips as his hands roamed her body, over the swell of her breasts, down the smooth valley in between, around the curve of her hips and along her soft thighs. Her breathing hitched as his hands skimmed over her clothes.

When his flat palm met her stomach, a low moan rippled through her body with a shudder. It had been too long since he'd been inside her, since he'd last kissed her like she was his forever and no one else ever would.

Desperation, urgency, a feral need to have her naked and

spread out underneath him had him bending at the knees to scoop her into his arms. She clutched his face with both hands and kissed him as though the same super-charged fuel coursed through her veins, too.

At the side of the bed, he sneezed and dropped her onto the mattress. "Shit, sorry."

She waved a hand at him through her giggles. "Don't be. You'd be far sorrier if you'd actually sneezed *on* me."

Warmth skittered up his neck and into his cheeks. "Point taken."

"Get naked." Her chin tilt and the desire sparkling in her eyes had him undressed in record time.

He creased his nose. "I'm stinky."

She nodded. "No lies detected."

"Can I shower first?"

She rolled her eyes but nodded again. "Be quick." She slid her hand down the front of her denim shorts. "You have less than three minutes."

Fuck. Was she kidding? Her hand moved lower and her breath caught. Nope. She wasn't kidding. His dick stirred and part of him wanted to say screw the shower, or drag her in for a bubbly scrub with him, but he was determined to take his time with her, to savor every breath, every whimper.

The last thing he wanted was for her to have to find the strength to stand upright in the shower. If they ever renovated the bathroom, he would strongly advocate for a bench in there.

He'd never washed so fast in all his life. It was just long enough to scrub off the thin film of grime from an afternoon in the yard, but not long enough to convince his cock to settle the fuck down. By the time he got back to her room, she was under the covers and her clothes were in a heap on the floor next to the bed.

Her cheeks were flushed. Her writhing had escalated. And

if he was a betting man, he'd guess she was pretty close to hitting the jackpot without him. Not on his watch.

He grabbed the end of the quilt and yanked it from her body but she didn't stop. Spreading her legs by her ankles, he nestled himself between her thighs and pushed them even farther apart. Her chest rose and fell heavily as her fingers slowed to lazy circles around her clit, his dick hardening underneath him.

"You're going to have to move your hand if you want me to take over." He slid a finger through her soft, soaking pussy and inside her, then two more and pressed hard against her front wall. The tremor that passed through her body was almost as good as the guttural sound that stuck in the back of her throat. "Let me make you feel good, CeeCee."

Dragging his tongue down the length of her slit, he hummed. He'd never get tired of her sweet saltiness, or the softness of her lips. He worked his fingers against her G-spot. As much as he wanted to bury himself inside her and pound her senseless, she deserved the world, and while it felt like he was going to blow his load at any moment, he needed to put her first.

He lapped at her clit with a flat tongue before teasing it with the very tip. Her hips bucked against his face, making him lick even harder. He loved how unhindered she was under his touch. She cried out, her fingers threading through his hair and gripping his face to her pussy. A burst of cool liquid met his face, but he didn't stop.

"Oh...my God...did... Fuck, Elliott. Fuck. Did I just squirt on you?"

She had, and he fucking loved it.

With a grunt he pressed harder against her G-spot, the sensitive spot providing little resistance as it softened under his touch, her pants and mewls lighting a fire under him to make her orgasm the best she'd ever had. Another squirt. Another "Oh my God."

Her nails bit into his scalp while her hips reared against his face. Her body tensed as she screamed his name and covered his face with her cum. Wiping his dripping mouth with the back of one hand, he grabbed her thigh and tugged her down the bed with the other.

He didn't give her time to recover before he inched his rock hard cock through her slick, glistening folds once... twice...and rammed it into her until he was balls deep and every ounce of tension left his body. She cried out again, and his hips found a jerky rhythm.

"Yes, baby. You did squirt on me." He wasn't going to last long. Hissing through gritted teeth he gripped her harder, fighting the building pressure at the base of his spine and the tightness swelling in his balls. "And it was the hottest fucking thing I've ever seen." Another thrust. A tingle at the bottom of his back. Fuck. He was going to be a two-pump chump for the love of his goddamned life, and he wasn't even sure he cared.

"I'm about to lose my shit right now. But I promise I'll recover quickly and do better the next time." He pushed again, and she clenched her muscles around his cock, shoving him over the edge into the blissful abyss.

"Fuck, Clare!"

She grinned up at him as he filled her, clutching her perfectly peach-shaped ass cheeks hard enough to leave marks. When he collapsed over her she poked at his ribs until he rolled off her and settled by her side.

"That was...quick."

She wasn't giggling or grinning, her voice was heavy with lust as she picked his hand up and draped it over her breast.

Circling her dusty rose nipple with his index finger, he kissed her shoulder before licking his lips. He tasted of her, her cum, her sweat, her perfume. "Sorry. I couldn't contain myself. It has just been too long since I've been inside you and…" He dropped his forehead to her shoulder with an awkward laugh, his face burning.

"No need to apologize, Eli. It was hot as fuck."

His head snapped up. Searching her face for signs of humor, he found none. "Really?"

She nodded. "A guy being unable to control himself during make-up sex? Hell yeah, it's fucking hot." Her hand curled around his dick and pumped, making a bead of cum trickle down the head and his toes to curl as he grunted. "But I want you again. So I'm gonna need you to get hard for me."

As she pumped his cock, he cupped her face and kissed her, deep and slow, but with every ounce of love he held for her in his heart. Rolling back over on top of her, he sighed against her mouth before pulling back to look at her.

He pushed her sweaty hair back from her face and dropped a kiss on the tip of her nose. "I love you, Clare. I've loved you since the day you kicked my shin in grade school. I loved you every single time I stepped out onto the ice, and I've loved you every goddamn day since."

"I love you, too." Tears trickled down her temples as she nibbled on her lip. "I'm sorry," she whispered. "I know crying during sexy time isn't exactly…well…sexy." She closed her eyes and more tears fell.

"If you're doing it right, the feels hit like a ton of bricks. I get it." He shushed her as he dotted kisses on her salty damp cheeks, then captured her lips with his once again. "I promise I'm never leaving you again."

Her arms tightened around his shoulders, bracing him against her with such force as she nodded. "You better not." She sniffed, and it cracked his heart in two. He'd been such a fucking idiot and hurt her so badly for so long.

But he'd change their narrative.

He'd make things better for her.

He'd be the man she needed him to be, the dependable guy who was always by her side, pushing her to do the big and scary things when she couldn't see the greatness in herself.

He kissed her with promise as he stroked her cheek. She was it for him. She'd always been it for him. Now he just needed to convince her that he meant it.

Six Months Later

"Help." Elliott crammed his phone between his ear and shoulder and took in the shelves of brightly colored boxes in front of him. Why the fuck was there so much choice? Couldn't they have a section of the store with a big fucking sign that said "Sent by your women to pick up period stuff? HERE IT IS."

Like a deer in headlights he was rooted to the spot. With so much choice how did women even choose? It's not like they could start at one end of the shelf and work their way through, testing each type along the way.

Hell no. At that price... He whistled. How the hell did women even afford to menstruate every month for the majority of their lives?

"You know if dudes had periods this shit would be free, right?"

"Uh huh." Clare's breathless voice came through the line. "They'd also come with free painkillers, a steak, and a coupon for an all body massage."

She wasn't wrong.

"Are you wrestling a bear?" He could almost hear her eye roll response.

"I'm moving the couch."

"The couch I told you to wait for me to be home to move?"

"I am a..." Huff. "Strong." Huff. "Independent." Huff. Huff. "Woman, goddammit." She punctuated the sentence with a heave and a frustrated growl. "I can do hard things by my big girl self."

A noise that sounded like her thumping the couch echoed down the line.

"Of course you can, CeeCee. But I'd really rather you didn't dislocate every bone in your entire spine trying to move a couch three times bigger than you. Just be patient."

She snarled at him—an honest to God snarl—and he couldn't help but smirk at her stubbornness. "Are you going to give me some direction here?"

"I dunno, Eli-Belly. I'm enjoying your blustering and in-store embarrassment right now. I might just leave you stuck in the period aisle of Walgreens for the rest of your life."

"Small problem being you actually need period supplies soooo..."

Another man joined him in the aisle, hands tucked into his back pockets as he scanned the shelves in awkward silence.

"Get Always Infinity. Regular flow. Please and thank you."

"And Cat?"

"She's good, thanks though."

With a nod, he hung up. As awkward as he felt shopping for women's *things*, he couldn't imagine what it was like for them to actually bleed for days every fucking month, still rock their lives like total queens, and not kill anyone.

For as strong as he was, papercuts brought him to his knees, he'd straight up die if he had periods. Reaching for the Clare-approved box of pads, he paused. "Just call her, man."

The man next to him shook his head.

With a sigh, Elliott picked up the pads. "My girlfriend says these are good, in case that helps."

The stranger didn't meet his eyes, his bright red face stayed pointed straight ahead, but he nodded. Wordlessly, he grabbed two boxes of the same kind of pads Clare had told Elliott to get, turned on his heels, and fled.

Next time Elliott was sent to the store for *provisions*, he was going to bring Mason with him. Someone needed to prepare the younger generation for the paralyzing fear of potentially bringing the wrong tampons home to their girlfriends.

It took him fifteen minutes to get back to Clare's, and the scents making their way down her front walk were enough to make him salivate. They'd been back together for only a matter of months, but turning up at her door for dinner was becoming a nightly thing. Despite the fact Cat was in college, and Mason was back and forth to his dad's, it felt like home. He didn't even knock anymore.

"Honey, I'm hoooooome!" He pushed the door open, unsuccessfully tried to dodge the blast of heat that smacked him in the face, and stepped inside.

In the kitchen, Clare basted an unusually large chicken. Mason chopped veggies to her left, and Cat worked the KitchenAid mixer on the island.

"Looks like I was out at just the right time. Avoiding all the hard work." He kissed Clare's sweaty temple and gave her waist a squeeze. "How was work?"

She'd started her new job a while ago, and though the transition from her old boss had been bumpy, the office at least sounded to be operating a little better with her at the helm. Not that he ever had any doubt.

"Exhausting."

"We could have ordered takeout."

She shook her head. "Not again. I refuse to eat another meal out of a bag this week."

Chuckling, he kissed her again. "It'll be better now that the season is over."

The Snow Pirates had gotten to the finals of the playoffs but fell at the last hurdle. As painful as it was to have lost in the last game, it was an overwhelming relief to know that the previous season hadn't been a fluke. He was, in fact, capable of putting together a championship deserving team.

And that felt pretty damn nice.

He reached over Clare's head to grab glasses from the cupboard. "White or red?"

"Either. Both. Just make it a big one. Skip the glass, just leave the bottle and a really long straw."

"Yes, ma'am." He winked at her and grabbed a bottle of white from the fridge. As he twisted the corkscrew, the doorbell chimed.

"I'll get it." An all-too-eager Cat abandoned her cheesecake making and made a beeline for the door. "Oh. It's you." Disappointment coated her words. "Come in. Mom, it's for you."

"Actually, I'm just here to give this back to Mason. He left it at my place last weekend." The Sperm Donor followed Cat into the kitchen. "Wow." He gestured around the room with Mason's helmet. "You've done a lot of work around here."

He caught Elliott's eye and with a tight smile, he gave a rigid nod. "The place looks great."

Clare wiped her hands on her yoga pants and nodded. "It's amazing what a fresh coat of paint will do to a room. Who knew?" Her already pink cheeks darkened as she cleared her throat and gave her best fake smile. "We're, uh, just about to eat. Would you like to join us?"

It had to be a fake smile—if it was any more brittle, her face would crack. The two kids did little to hide their surprise, but Elliott nodded along as though they'd planned the whole thing together and it was totally normal for Clare to be civil to The Sperm Donor.

What the fuck had come over her? Was this a distress signal? Had she been abducted by aliens?

The only way he could tell she was being polite was the tiny twitch at the corner of her mouth. Otherwise she looked completely relaxed and normal. He'd bet the house that it pained her to ask him, and she was quietly praying he'd say no.

"Thanks, but I gotta get back."

"Okay." Clare spun back to the worktop on a sigh, her shoulders softening. "See you next week."

The Sperm Donor hung around for another awkward beat before leaving. Elliott walked up behind her, placing his lips next to her ear. "Are you ill?"

An almost hysterical, nervous laugh shook her body. "I was trying to be nice."

"I thought you had temporarily taken leave of your senses."

"I'm so fucking glad he said no. Where's my wine?"

As he poured her an extra-large glass of Riesling, the doorbell rang again and Clare stiffened. "Fuck. Shit. Fuckety fuck. Please tell me he's not back again. I really wasn't serious about him actually eating a meal with us. Poisoning someone is still considered bad form, right?"

"And it's illegal." Elliott laughed and turned to answer the door, but Cat was already pushing past him. "I got it!"

She flung the door open with gusto and a grin. "You came."

A bashful Theo with a bright red face stood on the doorstep with two bunches of flowers and a gift bag. What the fuck was he doing there?

"You invited me."

Oh, she had, had she? The plot thickened. From the love

hearts popping out of Cat's head, she hadn't invited him to give Mason hockey tips.

Danger. Danger, Will Robinson. Elliott could *feel* Clare's scowl without even looking her direction.

Oooooooh boy.

"Yesssss! Best dinner, ever!" Mason fist pumped, his grin wide.

A frown pinched Clare's face as she walked toward Theo. "Theo. What a lovely surprise."

The kid's eyes bugged out. "Su-surprise? Cat said..." His head swung to Cat. "You said!"

"I told you I might invite someone to dinner, Mom." The Reynold's eye-rolling gene was strong with this one.

"Come in out of the doorway, rookie. Dinner will be ready in a few." Elliott ushered him into the house and closed the door behind him and Cat mouthed "Thank you" behind Theo's back.

"Th-these are for you, Mrs. Reynolds. Thanks for having me." Theo handed Clare one of the two bouquets and turned to Cat. "And these are for you."

The flowers definitely helped soften the ground with Clare. While she tried to hide her smile behind the Gerber daisies and roses, Elliott still caught it as she turned back to the counter.

"I'll grab a vase." He dug under the sink and as his hand curled around the cool, glass lip of a vase, a loud beeping made him start and crack his head on the edge of the cupboard. "The fuck?"

"Shit! Shit! Shit!"

Rubbing the back of his head, he stood into a plume of acrid smoke quickly filling the kitchen.

"I turned the broiler on to crisp the bacon on top of the chicken. I guess with the revolving door of visitors, I forgot about it." She rescued the charred chicken from the oven and placed it next to the sink as Cat fanned the smoke with a cloth.

Elliott opened the window and Theo stood—still holding his gift bag—wincing as the smoke alarm's wails continued.

"What about it we—?"

Clare jabbed a finger at him. "Don't you dare say it, Elliott Swift. Don't you fucking dare."

Mason flashed a grin and Cat rolled her lips between her teeth.

"Say what?" Theo looked between Elliott and Clare, then back to Cat.

Elliott shrugged. "Take out."

Epilogue
ELLIOTT

(One Year Later)

"Big day today, Coach." Theo slapped Elliott on his shoulder and gave a squeeze. "Got your game face on?"

Elliott shook his head. "She told you?"

"She's my girl, Coach. She tells me everything."

Elliott slowly turned to face Theo who threw his hands up in surrender. "Okay, fine. She doesn't tell me *everything*. But she told me this, yes."

"Which this?"

Theo checked over both shoulders. "The proposal." He checked again. "And the house closes today, right?"

His gut swirled. She'd told him both things. So she'd basically told him everything. With a sigh, Elliott shrugged. "Maybe I should give it a bit more time. Maybe I—"

Theo patted his chest. "It's cool, Coach. I make a great wing man. Today's the day. The *right* day. You get to cut the last tie to your past and finally put a ring on your future. It's all good."

While it wasn't quite the smack upside the head Dad would have given, the kid also wasn't wrong. Dad. He rubbed his chest with a clenched fist. It had been six months since Mom had passed peacefully in her sleep, and less than twenty-four hours later, Dad had died, too.

Elliott had always known that when the time came for one of his parents to let go, it wouldn't be long for the other one to pass away either. They didn't know how to live without each other, nor did they want to.

A love to last the ages. That's what his parents had, it was what he had with Clare, and Theo was right. It was the right day to put a ring on it. He should have done it the moment he'd come back into her life, but he needed to prove he was worthy first.

"You have the paint?"

"Yes, Coach. It's already on the ice. Enzo says snacks and merch are both ready. Seb says the team is down on the ice. Doors open in ten."

With the loss of two heavyweights on the team, Lincoln and Russell at the end of the previous season when they graduated, Elliott had—once again—been faced with the insurmountable task of filling their skates on the roster.

Mercifully, Theo and Enzo had both stepped up and were coming into their own. They had both turned out to be quite dependable. And despite the fact Theo was *still* dating "Coach's daughter," things weren't half bad.

"Got the ring?" Though he had a tendency to be a relentless pain in the ass.

"Yes, Theo. I have the ring."

Theo's phone chimed. "Cat says they're pulling up outside." He bounced on the balls of his feet. "I've never painted the ice before. I mean, I've seen NHL teams do it at the end of the season, but I've never done it myself, y'know?"

Elliott arched a brow. "You realize it's more for the fans than for the players, right?"

"Huh?" Theo frowned. "What? Oh. Yeah. Yes. Totally. No reason we can't have fun with it too, right, Coach?"

Elliott leveled him with a hard stare. "If so much as one of my players draws anything remotely phallic, or cusses in paint on that ice, so help me—"

"Elliott?" Cat's accusing voice echoed through the corridor behind him.

Theo held his hands up again. "No, Sir. Nothing phallic, no cussing. We know." His voice was a hushed whisper.

"Elliot." Cat advanced toward him, an outstretched index finger pointed in his direction. "What are you doing to my poor boyfriend?"

Theo gave a nervous laugh. "Nothing, baby. Misunderstanding. Right, Coach? Right." He rushed forward and grabbed Cat's hand. "Let's go down to the ice, the team is already there." He gave a thumbs up to Elliott, smiled at Clare, and bolted with Cat and Mason by his side.

"That kid is...strange." Clare jerked her thumb over her shoulder. "Stranger than normal, maybe. Is he okay?"

He nodded, his tongue suddenly three sizes too big for his mouth. It was almost time to ask her the biggest question of his life, and while he was sure she wanted it as much as he did, there was still a tiny voice in his head that said she'd say no.

"Are *you* okay?" She cupped his jaw and studied his face. "Nervous about the closing? Don't be. It's all going to be okay. They'll buy the house, you'll get your cut, and you'll be free of Denise and Tim once and for all." She paused and blew out a huff of air. "I can't believe she's pregnant again so soon. Two kids so close together..." She shuddered. "It's not easy. Especially with Tim being back at work. It's going to be tough for her."

He nodded, but he didn't really want to talk about his ex.

He was glad she'd truly moved on with her life and they had little to do with each other unless it was to do with the sale of the house. That period of his life was almost over for good.

With Clare and the team's help, he'd already gutted out and sold his parent's house in the past year. Surviving that had been painful. He wasn't really worried that the sale of his previous home would fall through, but it helped for Clare to believe it—then she wouldn't pry about what was really bothering him.

By the time they got down to the ice pad, clusters of fans had made their way out onto the ice. Ticket holders had been invited to use the ice as a cold canvas to spread messages and create art.

Brushes in hand, fans got to painting. Drawings of current and past players were added to the ice, along with "thank you" messages written to the players for their performances during the season.

Some fans left behind their own stories, leaving names and even playing tic-tac-toe. But none of that mattered—not really. He swallowed as he stood up from his own creative masterpiece and dusted off his knees.

He nodded at Cat. It was a terrible "go" signal, but they figured anything more obvious might draw suspicion from Clare. Cat stood behind her mom and covered her eyes with both hands before shuffling her across the ice toward Elliott.

Taking a knee, he settled in place before pulling the small, velvet ring box from his pocket and sending up a prayer.

"Can't I look yet? I'm sure Mason doesn't mind his painting not being completely perfect." Clare wriggled in Cat's grasp.

"Just another sec, Mom. Be patient." Cat beamed down at Elliott who nodded again.

When she pulled her hands from Clare's eyes, it took her a moment to adjust and react. She blinked rapidly before her

EPILOGUE

gaze settled on the ring in his hand. Her eyes flicked between the ring box in his hand, to the message painted in blue paint next to him on the ice.

Will you marry me, Clare?

"Oh my God." She glanced around the ice, and likely to no one's surprise, all eyes were on them.

"What do you say, CeeCee? Will you be mine forever?"

Cat clapped her hands like an excited seal before wiping her tears with the side of her hand.

"Of course I'll marry you!" She rushed forward and reached for him.

Heaving his weight off the ice, he grunted as he stood. "I'm too old for this shit."

"I hope not. I want at least another forty years with you, Coach."

Plucking the ring from its plush cushion, he smiled, then hesitated. "You sure?"

"Put the ring on my finger already, old man." Her grin could have powered the huge screen mounted over center ice. And as he slid the ring onto her finger, the crowd erupted into cheers and applause.

He pulled her to him, cradling her chin, and as he dipped his head to kiss her, players and fans rushed over to pat him on the back and congratulate them.

While the handshakes and well wishes continued, out of the corner of his eye Enzo and Theo stood chatting. "That'll be you next, right Theo-dear?"

The color drained from Theo's face as realization dawned that Elliott had heard what his friend had said.

Elliott pointed a finger at the young man. "Over my dead body, kid. Finish college first, you hear me?"

"Y-yes, sir. A-absolutely Coach. I would never."

"Damn straight, you would never."

Clare patted his chest. "Leave the boy alone, Elliott. Don't you remember what it's like to be young and in love?"

Bending at the knee, he threw her a grin before picking her up and tossing her over his shoulder. "What do you mean, remember?" He slapped her butt cheek. "I'm still young, and I'm still madly in love with you. I'll give you *old man*."

Her giggles shook her body as he carried her toward the edge of the rink.

"I'm taking the future Mrs. Swift out for lunch. You're in charge, Enzo. Don't mess up."

"Yes, Coach. I got you."

Theo smacked Enzo's chest and the two started roughhousing. Cat gave Mason a hug before he ran over to his dad who was crouched low to the ice holding a brush.

Elliott slid Clare to her feet when he got her off the ice. She worked her bottom lip between her teeth and grabbed his arm, tugging him down the corridor. "You sure we don't have time for a quickie in your office first, Coach?"

As he followed her to his office, he couldn't help but smile. He could be the future Mr. Clare Reynolds and couldn't fucking wait.

She rolled the ring around under the light as she walked. "It's gorgeous, Eli. Did you think about when we might... y'know...?"

She closed the door behind him and stared at the ring again.

"Tomorrow? Next week? Next month? How long do we really need? Hell, let's go to City Hall right now and seal the deal. I don't want to wait another fucking second." With every word he spoke, he advanced on her, boxing her against the wall with flat palms on either side of her head.

"I don't think that's quite how it works, Coach." She brushed her lips against his. "But I can confirm your enthusiasm is getting me all hot under the hood."

"Then let me give you a damn good time, Future Mrs. Swift." He slipped his hand down the front of her jeans. "And when you're done whimpering my name as you come, we'll go get married."

Not ready to leave Clare and Elliott just yet? That's okay, I have a bonus epilogue waiting just for you!

Want to know what happened during the pre-season between the Snow Pirates and the Raccoons? Find out here in the crossover novella Two for Tacos: books2read.com/twofortacos

Keep reading for a sneak peek of book 1 in the Cedar Rapids Raccoons series. Books2read.com/freezingthepuck

CHAPTER 22
Savannah

I can't decide.

Chris-bean-a Aguilera, or Queen Latte-fah?

I've been staring at the menu for longer than is considered socially acceptable, and I still can't decide. I'm going to order what I always do. I know it. The Barbie-pink haired barista giving me sympathetic eyes knows it. And my best friend, Athena, sitting at our usual table shooting daggers into my back while she waits for me to order her first caffeine hit of the day, knows it, too. Hell, even the hero and heroine in the romance novel I'm hugging against my chest know it.

Huh. Perhaps not. Bitches Brew—the best coffee shop in town—has added new things to their menu. The Cocoa Chanel looks drool-worthy. Buttery hot chocolate with hot pink whipped cream, mini marshmallows, and edible glitter.

Ooooh. Come to mama.

But what if it's not as good as it looks on the menu board?

Nothing is ever as good as it looks on the menu board. And it's quite the beautiful-looking menu board. Everything in the coffee shop is pretty: striking, hot pink, and sparkly. First appearances come with a pink punch at Bitches Brew.

There's so much interesting *stuff*, like a pink guitar hanging from the ceiling and a pink bike mounted on the wall over a fireplace, that I almost get distracted by it all and forget I'm supposed to be ordering.

Almost. I need to focus. Turning my attention back to the menu board, I shift my weight. I need to pick something to order. It shouldn't be this hard.

But I *know* my Ruth Bader-Brewsburg, their dark chocolate mocha, is delicious. I love the depth of the coffee flavor, the richness of the chocolate, and how Taryn—my favorite barista and owner of Bitches Brew—takes the time to draw a music staff and notes with cocoa powder on top of my drink.

I do this every time. Every fucking time.

I convince myself that I'm going to stray from my boring, same old, same old and try something new. It's on the tip of my tongue, venturing out from my safe space into the unknown. But the comforting familiarity of my old favorite sinks its claws into me, just a little deeper, and I can't stop myself from blurting out the same thing I always get.

I know one thing, though. If I don't hurry up and bring Athena her Ariana Grande with an extra shot of Espresso Patronum, they're never going to find my body.

"You ready to order?" Taryn flashes me her superstar grin. I've been coming to Bitches Brew for as long as I've been a student at the University of Cedar Rapids, Iowa, AKA: UCR. Three years. And for three years I've ordered the same thing, every single time.

Maybe today, first day of my third and senior year, is The Day.

I nod and suck in a breath. "I'll have an Ariana Grande with an extra shot." A quick glance over my shoulder tells me that Athena has hit DEFCON 2.

She's starting her junior year. We met right here at the coffee shop, on our first day of college three years ago when she tried to hit on me. I was flattered, but I'm straight. She took it in stride, we got to talking, and the rest is BFF history.

She's the Geena Davis to my Susan Sarandon, the Buffy to my Willow, the Christina Yang to my Meredith Grey.

A grunt, and a string of Spanish profanities indicates she's escalated to DEFCON 1. "Better make it two extra shots, please, Taryn."

Her perfectly curled pink hair bobs up and down as she nods. "And for you?" She arches a manicured brow like she's expecting me to say something different, something new. I can't blame her, I've spent more time than usual examining her new board.

I meet her eyes, warmth blooming in my cheeks. How in the name of all that's holy does she get her eyeliner flicks so even?

The gaggle of geese hanging out around the small lake outside are honkin' up a storm. Even they know what I'm gonna order.

I heave out a sigh. Today isn't the day. "Ruth, please."

Her smile softens as she nods again. "You got it. Anything else?"

She's right. DEFCON 1 requires sugar as well as caffeine. "Hen will take the lady lips, and I'll have a dick waffle dipped in white chocolate. Please and thank you."

There's no judgment in Taryn's eyes. It's one of the reasons Bitches Brew is so popular, it's a safe space for all. A hot pink, glitz-and-glam safe space. I should be in charge of their marketing with such original taglines.

You wanna eat a dozen twat waffles and wash it down with a gallon of coffee? No judgment.

You do you, boo.

We can also work for six hours straight and use the free Wi-Fi when we are behind on projects and are butting up against deadlines. That one might be oddly specific to me, though somehow I doubt it.

Here, people can be their most authentic selves, without apologies. A twinge catches in my chest making my breath stutter. I don't really know who my most authentic self is anymore.

I thought I knew my most authentic self. I thought—I don't know what I thought—but finding the piece of paper in my dad's study telling me that I wasn't born a Bowen, that I'd been adopted as an infant and my parents hadn't told me? That shook me to my core.

It still shakes my core. I've spent the months since trying to figure out who I really am. I'd love to say that piece of paper didn't define me, or that it didn't change a single thing, but it did.

It changed everything.

I no longer know who I am. I tap my card against the machine and smile through the pain shredding my insides. My parents—my *adoptive* parents—kept it from me for almost twenty years. I've only known for a couple of months. But... How can I not be changed now that I know the truth?

The almost unhappy beep of the machine suggests a problem, and I scowl, wrinkles creasing my forehead. "Can you run it again please?"

Taryn nods and hits a couple buttons before I flap my card against the end of the machine one more time. Heat creeps up my spine and into my extremities. I place my book on the counter—cover up, because there's no shame in my smut of choice game. I know Taryn loves my hot as hell man-chest-candy covers as much as I do—then my purse.

Shit. If the card is declined again I don't think I have another way to pay.

I purged my bag last night so it was ready to collect receipts, tubes of Chapstick, and crumbs from food I don't eat anywhere near my purse. I thought I tossed my coin purse back into my bag, but the sinking feeling in my chest has me wondering if I left it at home.

Checking again, I confirm it. My coin purse is on my nightstand, right next to my charging vibrator and my half-empty glass of water. I close my eyes and send up a prayer. The Big Guy won't let me down. Right?

The same "transaction denied" sound scrapes my ears and my stomach drops.

I could ask Athena to front me the cash. It's my turn to buy, but she won't mind. Being the daughter of a billionaire, I know she has the dough. But I've taken pride in being that person—you know, the one who knows who she is but who doesn't want her for her money, or her family connections, or to get close to her delicious, hockey-playing brothers.

I love her for her. Not her last name.

"It's okay, I got it." A deep, velvety voice behind me sends a ripple through my body, sparking my lady bits to life.

Huh. I'd thought after all the months of neglect, apart from the occasional buzz with a battery operated boyfriend, that she'd closed up shop. Yet here she is reacting to a tall, dark, and handsome stranger behind me in line at the coffee shop. He has to be tall, dark, and handsome, right? With a voice like maple syrup, he must be.

A glance at my book cover confirms it—this is my very own meet-cute. Maybe he's even shirtless already.

Guy saves girl from embarrassment by offering to buy her coffee. A little clichéd, it's true, but I can totally work with clichéd. Especially if he has a romance-novel-hero sized dick.

I kinda wish I'd shaved my legs this morning. Because of course I'm going from meet-cute to mounting the hottie behind me in zero-point-three seconds.

I spin around, ready to say "I do" and cut right to my

happily ever after, and my jaw drops. Sure, he's tall, blond—not dark—and he's handsome alright, but he's also—

"You can insert or tap." Taryn's voice barely registers from behind me.

My hand darts out, blocking his card from touching the machine. "It's fine. I'll just... I'm sure I have cash in here somewhere." I jiggle my bag at him like that'll somehow make him disappear, an alternative method of payment appear, or my vision come into focus, and it won't be who I think it is, who I know it is, standing in front of me.

Instead, my *actual* not-a-douche-canoe knight in shining armor will be here to save me from caffeine withdrawal and a murderous best friend instead.

His brow arches high over his crystal blue eyes as he gives me that lopsided, jock smile that dazzles like a disco ball and makes women's underwear spontaneously combust. But the acid in my empty stomach bubbles, stomping out any desire I felt when I first heard his voice. Before I realized who it was.

I'd rather saw my arm off than let Justin Ass pay for my breakfast.

I blink. Try to restart my brain, but his blue eyes won't let go of me, and I don't move my hand from the card machine. The walls are closing in around us at a snail's pace, like a slow-motion 80's montage in a movie, and I'm pretty sure everyone is staring at me, staring at him, waiting for me to say or do something, or even just move.

Taryn clears her throat behind me. "Girl. Sometimes you gotta let the patriarchy pay for your coffee. Call it reparations." She moves the machine from my grasp and lets Justin tap the end. I'm still staring, mouth gaping, like another brainless idiot who loses the power of speech when a pretty hockey boy looks her way.

I look to the ceiling, to the Big Guy. This isn't funny.

Justin Ashe isn't my romance novel hero. He's not my happy ever after.

He's heartburn after a bad burrito.

He's always been the pretty boy, ever since high school. But his shoulders have filled out, and his biceps are stretching the navy-blue sweater as though it could burst at the seams like a can of Pillsbury biscuits.

I mumble an apology and a thank you—or at least I hope that's what came out of my mouth—and move to the side, fixing my eyes on...something...anything that isn't the man who paid for our drinks. His stare is heavier on my back than caffeine-thirsty Athena's was, and my cheeks are scorching.

What the fuck is he even doing here anyway?

Here. In *my* coffee shop.

In my fucking space.

He belongs back home, in Minnesota. Not here in Iowa. He's out of place, like a distant memory showing up out of context. Blindsided, bumfuzzled, betrayed. Ugh. I smooth down my shirt, even though it doesn't need to be smoothed. Every cell in my body wants me to haul ass out the door but I know he'd probably follow and make a scene.

Has he been going to UCR this whole time and I had no idea? I've been to a couple of hockey games over the years but I can't remember seeing him on the ice. Does he still play?

What the fuck is going on right now?

I get it, everyone is welcome in Bitches Brew, but as soon as I get the chance I'm going to add "except Justin-fucking-Ashe" in sharpie to the "Everyone Welcome" sign hanging on the front door. Yeah, it's also pink.

"You forgot your book."

My man-chest cover slides into view as Justin's outstretched arm offers me my novel. I want my fucking money back. J.R. Blake, my favorite romance author, has a lot to answer for. This isn't what was supposed to happen. *Justin* is *not* my fucking hero.

Except he kind of is since he just bought not only my caffeine, but Hen's too, and he's returning my current read.

He steps in front of me, still holding the book, giving it a wiggle as though to attract my attention. My face burns hotter as amusement and knowing dances in his gaze. Jerk. So I like some on-page spice with my love stories, it's no big deal.

I could be a murderer. Or worse, I could be someone who leaves her toenail clippings next to the bathroom sink. What's a little bit of sex between the covers? I'm a consenting adult. Or at least I would be if I could find my very own fucking hero.

Justin is still smirking at me. Judgmental asshat.

I snatch the book from his grasp and jam it into my purse. A frown pinches his flawless face, and he purses his lips.

Shit. My stomach tightens. Does he think we're going to talk now? To start a conversation at the counter while I wait for my drinks?

Hard pass.

Hundred percent not going to happen, buddy. Just because you saved me from certain death with Athena for further delayed caffeination doesn't mean we're in some way even-steven. Not even close.

I toss a look at Taryn, convinced she's stalling, taking longer than she normally would to make the drinks, to give me time to talk to the pretty-boy hockey player still scowling at me.

Doesn't he remember me?

Another twitch in my stomach. Fuck.

Wouldn't that be the kick-in-the-crotch cherry on top? We went to the same high school. Hell, we even ran in the same circles for years. I haven't changed all that much. Not enough for him not to recognize me. Unless I really was that unmemorable to him.

Fuck.

Does he really not know who I am?

I'm not sure what I want more—him to remember me, or to forget I ever existed. One thing's for certain, though, I am *not* getting into a conversation with this man. I don't care how pretty his eyes are, or how my nether regions react to the gravelly timbre of his voice.

Once bitten, twice shy—that's the old adage, right?

Justin Ashe took a chunk out of my best friend...out of *me* in high school. And while I'm not shy, exactly, bet your ass I'm not giving him the chance to do it again. I narrow my eyes. Maybe I can scare him away by trying to emulate Athena's resting bitch face. She is the master of saying everything she needs to with just an icy stare.

I'm pretty sure my face is as bright pink as the Bitches Brew décor, but my insides are as black as the accent walls. I need this guy out of my space.

He opens his mouth to speak, and Taryn announces my order is ready at the end of the coffee bar. Thank fuck for that.

If he'd said anything to me, I'm not sure what I'd have done. The only words I have for him are venom-coated and fuelled by the misdirected anger simmering in my veins. Maybe not so misdirected. Sure, I've been pissed at my parents —adoptive parents—for months, but my rage at Justin Ashe has spanned years and feels just as acute as it did back in high school.

He's deserving of my burning rage. Even if he looks...like *that*.

I gratefully accept the tray from Taryn and grunt my thanks once again at Douchebag Magee before I make my way to Athena like a T-rex is chasing me for my dick waffle. Silly T-rex. Everyone knows I never share my dick waffles.

"We're leaving." The long strap of my purse slips over the curve of my shoulder and slides down my arm, making the bag land on the floor at my feet with a heavy thud like it's punctuating my sentence. With the tray balanced in both hands, I can't pick it up yet, so I shift my toes toward it like my foot can communicate my irritation that it fell. My bangs are in my eyes, and my skin is on fire.

I feel his gaze on my body, probing, curious, amused.

Athena sits back in her chair and tosses me a smirk. "You're holding plates. Are we stealing plates? I don't think Taryn would let us back if we steal her shit."

I groan. She's right. Taryn did me dirty. She always gives us paper cups so we can eat and run, but today? Today she's given us the oversized, not at all portable mugs. Dammit. The pink-haired cupid is way off the mark with her arrow this morning. I want to take the sharp-ended weapon and shove it up Justin's ass.

I place the tray onto the table with slightly too much force, and push my bangs out of my irritated eyeballs.

After a long sip of her coffee, Athena jerks her chin at what I assume is Justin still standing at the counter behind me. "Wanna talk about that?"

I'd rather sever my own carotid artery and watch myself bleed to death on the floor of the coffee shop. I pick up my chocolate-covered dick waffle and lick off the white chocolate jizz at the top before taking a huge bite and pointing to my mouth as if to say, "can't talk, eating."

"Found out anything about your birth parents yet?"

My girl is persistent, I'll give her that.

I point to my mouth again.

Chewing very studiously, I pull out my phone and open the local classifieds. I've searched every single day over the summer for a job. I want a job. I *need* a job. I need *something* to do outside of school, not only for the cash, but so I can avoid going back home to Minnesota as much as possible, to my parents—my adoptive parents. Something that gives me a legitimate reason to ignore my phone when their name flashes on the screen. Something to distract me from the hurricane of feelings tearing up my mind.

I shift in my seat and swear I can feel the pressure of his stare against my back. Something must show on my face because Hen raises an eyebrow.

"It's okay. We've all had crushes on hockey players before." She pats my hand, condescension and knowing hanging in the air between us. I wonder who she's talking about having had a crush on. She hates hockey. Having brothers living and breathing the sport turned her off it long ago—or so she says. Maybe there's another reason she won't step into the rink to watch a game. That's a thread that'll need to be pulled on in the future.

She picks up her lady lips pastry and drags her tongue across the seam before making moaning sexy sex noises at its deliciousness. She's tongue fucking the slit right there in front of me, in front of everyone.

"People are staring." I'm convinced the dude at Athena's three o'clock is going to come in his pants if she doesn't stop putting on a show.

She teases where the clit would be—if it were *real* lady lips—with the tip of her tongue, and the dude groans. Her smirk only grows.

"I don't have a crush on anyone." I take another bite of my dick before my high school self claws out of the box in my chest and spills the ancient history tea to my best friend.

Some things need to remain in the past, and Justin-fucking-Ass is one of them.

Click here to keep reading Justin and Savannah's book, Freezing the Puck

Author Note

Funny story, y'all: When this series came to me in a flash of delightful inspiration, I had zero intention of writing Coach Swift's story. Zero. I had a plan. I had covers and characters, I had tropes and God damnit I even had outlines. I was ready to be an organized and serious author.

Bahahahahaha. And I would have gotten away with it, too, if it wasn't for those pesky kids.

With each book I wrote, I became more intrigued by Elliott's story. Where had he come from? What was his deal? I put it on the back burner and said, okay, I'll write that someday. Maybe. Except characters never do what we want them to, right? They talk to us when they need to, not when we might want them to, and they take our best laid plans and shit all over them.

Just like Elliott and Clare did.

I haven't written a second chance romance since way back in AJ and Lisa's story, before I knew how to write a book in line with reader's expectations. And considering we had already met Clare in Austin and Kenzie's book, the two started chittering at me like they'd known each other their whole lives. Funny that, eh?

It was important to me when writing this book to capture the essence of a single working mom. For those of you reading who have kids—whether you're a stay at home parent, or a working parent, I'm sure you see pieces of yourself in Clare throughout the book. We do what we have to do to make sure the little people in our lives have everything they need—regardless of how old they are. Our kids are our kids and age doesn't matter—baby or teen.

But I have a couple of single parent working mom friends on my Facebook feed and they are off the chart with their commitment and dedication. How the hell they keep all their plates spinning without their heads actually spinning like something from The Exorcist is anyone's freakin' guess.

Those parents are the real MVP. They save themselves, their kids, and they do it with an (albeit tired) smile on their faces. They do it because they have to, because they have no choice, because the love they have for their kids surpasses every other kind of love there is in the whole world.

We'd walk through fire for our children. We'd go tired and hungry, slay dragons, and even battle math homework for our children. And most of the time it's a thankless job. They think we're mean, they leave their shit everywhere, and sometimes they throw tantrums that register on the Richter scale.

But every now and then they see us, really, truly see us and it's in those moments where we truly see how good of a job we've done in raising the little crotch goblins.

I dunno about y'all, but there's nothing I wouldn't do for my son—okay, sure, I hide my 3.5lb bag of Hot Tamales from him so he doesn't 'share.' And sure, I might sneak some of his fries occasionally, or say that somewhere is closed just 'cause I don't wanna go, but in the grand scheme of things, I'd do anything for him. And on the days when he's not grumping at me for being a buzzkill, I think he might even know it, too.

So this book is for all the exhausted parents who wonder every day if they're doing it right—You. Fucking. Are. Just keep going.

Acknowledgments

Lewis—you know, there isn't a single book in my back catalogue that my son hasn't had a hand in getting across the finish line and this one is no different. He crossed out each Post It like he'd written the words himself and when I reached the end after a long slog, he hi-fived me, hugged me, and told me to put up new ones so 'we' could start on the next one. He truly is my biggest supporter and without him I'd probably still be on my first book. I love you 3,000.

Tracie and Clare—you two got me through once again. From ass-crack-of-dawn sprints, to gin and Fanta in Madrid, this book carries part of all of us in the pages. Thanks for hauling my stubborn ass through the sticky parts, and for listening to my—very minor and only occasional—whining. You're both loved and appreciated more than you may realize, but since my four-ness is almost always on my sleeve, I should hope you at least have some idea at how much I heart you both.

Heather—Thank you for forcing me to stop and take a breath every now and then. For caring, for being my rock. It's so hard being alone, and feeling so lonely, even four years after coming back to NI, and without you giving a shit, I'm not sure I'd have made it this far.

My squad—you should know who you are. My new Irish sprint buddies, my new BFF Irene who I met in Madrid (she's basically the American version of me), my Goal Oriented Nagging buddies, and my OG 20Books friends. Thank you. Thank you for constantly inspiring me, for kicking me in the vagina when I need that extra shove, and for dragging me through when I am throwing a tantrum like a threenager and don't wanna adult. I couldn't do what I do without such an amazing chosen family.

My Alphas—Savannah, Amy R, Erika, Robynne and **My Betas**—Micky and Corinne. Where would I be without y'all, eh? I can probably take a guess considering how crippling my impostor syndrome can often be. Thank you all, for your feedback, for your encouragement, and for shouting about my books like every single one is your favorite.

Cally—I see you. You're a great mom. You are enough.

HUGE thanks to my editor Jessica Snyder, and my cover designer Kate Farlow over at Y'all That Graphic.

And finally, to my ARC readers, my Facebook reader group *Margaritas, Men, and Mischief with Lasairiona*, and to each and every one of you who pick up this book: a bazillion thank yous. I truly hope you loved it enough to pick up the next one. Tell your friends! And if you're not in my group —come join us, we don't bite (unless you ask us to!)

Also by Lasairiona McMaster

Two for Interference - Minnesota Snow Pirates book 1

Freezing the Puck - Cedar Rapids Raccoons book 1

Two for Tacos - A Snow Pirates Novella

Control - The Protocol Series (Writing as: Lasairiona Lewis)

www.Lasairiona.com

About the Author

Lasairiona McMaster writes sassy, classy and badassy women and strong, yet vulnerable men. She challenges reader's expectations by openly dealing with mental health issues, often exploring tough-to-handle topics and 'taboos' and books with a whole lotta heart.

She can either be found enjoying a gin and lemonade by the Irish sea, or baking sweet treats in her kitchen while singing at the top of her lungs. When she's 'home' in Texas, and isn't eating fresh-popped popcorn while buying things she has absolutely no need for in Target, she can be found at Chuys eating her body weight in chips and queso and washing it down with a margarita swirl. She loves to make friends out of strangers.

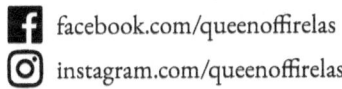

facebook.com/queenoffirelas
instagram.com/queenoffirelas

www.ingramcontent.com/pod-product-compliance
Lightning Source LLC
Chambersburg PA
CBHW030033100526
44590CB00011B/180